Fair and Equitable Treatment

International Investment Law and Arbitration

Volumes published in this Brill Research Perspectives title are listed at *brill.com/rpia*

Fair and Equitable Treatment

Its Interaction with the Minimum Standard and Its Customary Status

By

Patrick Dumberry

BRILL

LEIDEN | BOSTON

This paperback book edition is simultaneously published as issue 1.2 (2017) of *International Investment Law and Arbitration*, DOI 10.1163/24055778-12340002.

Library of Congress Control Number: 2018930626

Typeface for the Latin, Greek, and Cyrillic scripts: "Brill". See and download: brill.com/brill-typeface.

ISBN 978-90-04-36611-4 (paperback)
ISBN 978-90-04-36612-1 (e-book)

This book is printed on acid-free paper and produced in a sustainable manner.

Contents

Fair and Equitable Treatment: Its Interaction with the Minimum Standard and Its Customary Status

Patrick Dumberry
University of Ottawa
patrick.dumberry@uottawa.ca

Abstract

The book addresses two questions which have been debated by scholars in the last 20 years regarding the fair and equitable treatment ('FET') standard found in BITs. It examines the interaction between the 'minimum standard of treatment' (MST) and the FET standard. It first analyses the fascinating story of how the concept of the MST emerged in the early 20th Century, its subsequent decline from 1960s until the 1990s and its surprising recent 'resurrection' in the year 2000. This evolution has had a direct impact on the emergence and subsequent development of the FET standard and explains why States started referring to that standard instead of the MST in their investment treaties. One question addressed in this book, is whether FET is an autonomous standard of protection to be accorded to foreign investors, or is a mere reference to the MST under customary international law. Given the fact that the FET standard is found in the overwhelming majority of BITs, another question which arose is whether or not it should now be considered in and of itself as a rule of customary international law.

Keywords

fair and equitable treatment standard – minimum standard of treatment – customary international law – State practice – BITs

 | DOI 10.1163/9789004366121_002

General Introduction

In recent years, a number of books,[1] including one by the present author,[2] and numerous articles have been published on the fair and equitable treatment ('FET') standard. The standard is found in the overwhelming majority of BITS and has become in the last decades one of the most controversial provisions examined by arbitral tribunals. The aim of this publication is not to offer a comprehensive analysis of the scope and content of the FET standard. The goal is more modest. I want to address two of the many questions which have been debated by scholars in the last 20 years.

The first question examined in Chapter I is related to the interaction between the 'minimum standard of treatment' (MST) and the FET standard. It analyses the fascinating story of how the concept of the MST emerged in the early 20th Century, its subsequent decline from 1960s until the 1990s and its surprising recent 'resurrection' in the year 2000. This evolution has had a direct impact on the emergence and subsequent development of the FET standard. Thus, why have States started referring to the FET standard instead of the MST in their investment treaties? In answering this question, I will address the controversial question of whether the FET is an autonomous standard of protection to be accorded to foreign investors, or is a mere reference to the MST under customary international law.

The second question examined in Chapter II concerns the (alleged) customary status of the FET standard. Since FET clauses are now found in the overwhelming majority of BITS, should the standard be considered as a rule of customary international law? The present author recently published a book on how rules of customary international law are created and how they can be

1 Ioana Tudor, *The Fair and Equitable Treatment Standard in International Foreign Investment Law* (Oxford UP 2008); Gabriel Cavazos Villanueva, *The Fair and Equitable Treatment Standard: The Mexican Experience* (VDM Verlag 2008); Roland Kläger, *Fair and Equitable Treatment in International Investment Law* (Cambridge UP 2011); Alexandra Diehl, *The Core Standard of International Investment Protection: Fair and Equitable Treatment* (Wolters Kluwer 2012); Martins Paparinskis, *The International Minimum Standard and Fair and Equitable Treatment* (Oxford UP 2013); T. Weiler, *The Interpretation of International Investment Law: Equality, Discrimination and Minimum Standards of Treatment in Historical Context* (Martinus Nijhoff 2013); Andrea Schernbeck, *Der Fair and Equitable Treatment Standard in internationalen Investitionsschutzabkommen* (Nomos 2013).

2 Patrick Dumberry, *The Fair and Equitable Treatment Standard: A Guide to NAFTA Case Law on Article 1105* (Wolters Kluwer 2013).

identified in the field of international investment law.[3] The aim of this publication is to apply the findings of my book about how customary rules are created and to concretely 'test' them in the specific context of the FET standard.

I The Interaction between the 'Minimum Standard of Treatment' and the FET

Introduction

The first chapter of this book examines the question of the interaction between the MST and the FET standard.[4]

Section 1 examines the emergence of the MST in the early 20th century as a basic threshold of treatment meant to be imposed on all States and afforded to all *foreign* investors, notwithstanding the level of treatment already offered by States to their own nationals. In the 1920s and 1930s, international jurisprudence slowly developed the concept, and by the end of World War II it was well-established as a rule of custom. In the 1960s and 1970s, Newly Independent States began to challenge the existence of any such MST. While the standard ultimately survived these events, its opposition had another more subtle consequence: both developing and developed States now perceived the MST as ineffective in providing basic legal protection to foreign investors doing business abroad. It is in this historical context that both developed and developing States began frenetically signing bilateral treaties for the promotion and protection of investments ('BITS') that provided clearer rules on investment protection.

Section 2 examines the emergence of the FET standard in investment treaties and its interaction with the MST. One of the most controversial questions discussed in scholarship is why States began using the FET expression in their BITS instead of the well-established customary rule of the MST. According to one view, Western States incorporated the concept of FET into their BITS to simply reflect the MST that existed under international law. In other words,

3 P. Dumberry, *The Formation and Identification of Rules of Customary International Law in International Investment Law* (Cambridge UP 2016).

4 This chapter is a modified and up-to-date version of an earlier article published by the author: P. Dumberry, 'The 'Minimum Standard of Treatment' in International Investment Law: The Fascinating Story of the Emergence, the Decline and the Recent Resurrection of a Concept', in: Luca Pasquet, Klara Polackova Van der Ploeg, and Léon Castellanos Jankiewicz (eds), *International Law and Time: Narratives and Techniques: Proceedings of the Conference International Law and Time* (Springer, 2018).

the FET was simply used as a convenient, neutral and acceptable reference to the MST. A more convincing approach, however, explains that Western States started to use the expression *because* of the ambiguities surrounding the concept of the MST and the fact that it had been heavily contested by many States in the past. The drafting language used by States in their BITs supports this approach insofar as the vast majority of them contain stand-alone (or autonomous) references to the FET standard without mention of international law or the MST. In my view, the FET standard should *generally* be considered as an *independent* treaty standard with an autonomous meaning from the MST. Yet, there are some *particular situations* where this is not the case: when a treaty *explicitly* links the FET to the standard existing under 'international law' or the MST (one example is NAFTA Article 1105[5]).

In any event, by the end of the 1990s the MST, as a source of investment protection for foreign investors, was in sharp decline. Section 3 examines the phenomenon of the 'return' of the MST to center stage. Its return was the consequence of many tribunals (notably in the context of NAFTA) beginning to interpret FET clauses in the early 2000s and concluding that they provide investors with *more extensive* rights than under the MST. States reacted strongly to these controversial awards. For instance, NAFTA Parties issued a binding Note of Interpretation explaining that they had always intended for the FET standard to be interpreted strictly as a reference to the MST. NAFTA Parties, as well as a number of other States, also began to refer explicitly to the MST in FET clauses contained in their investment treaties. Their clear aim was to limit the scope of investors' rights under said clauses. The novel FET clause contained in the EU-Canada *Comprehensive Economic and Trade Agreement* (CETA), which includes a detailed list of the elements considered to be in breach of the standard, is clearly the most explicit attempt by States to achieve that goal.

1 *The Emergence of the MST as a Rule of Customary International Law*

The first section defines the concept of the MST and examines its customary status (Section 1.1.). The following sections examine its historical foundation (Section 1.2.) and the subsequent challenges to its customary status that was led by developing States in the 1960s and 1970s (Section 1.3.), which resulted in the new phenomenon of 'treatification' in the 1990s (Section 1.4.).

1.1 The Concept of the MST and Its Customary Status

Despite some disagreement between States on the existence of the MST in the last few decades (a point that will be examined further below), the concept

5 For an analysis of this provision, see: Dumberry (n 2).

is now predominantly recognized as a rule of customary international law. Many States have explicitly recognized the customary status of the MST in their pleadings in investment arbitration proceedings.[6] The customary nature of the MST has also been recognized by several NAFTA awards.[7] It has also been

---

6 See, for instance, the following (non-exhaustive) list of cases: *Azurix Corp v. Argentina*, ICSID Case No. ARB/01/12, Award, 14 July 2006 [332–333]; *Bayindir Insaat Turizm Ticaret ve Sanayi A Ş v. Pakistan*, ICSID Case No. ARB/03/29, Award, 27 August 2009 [164, 173]; *Bureau Veritas, Inspection, Valuation, Assessment and Control, BIVAC BV v. Paraguay*, ICSID Case No. ARB/07/9, Further Decision on Objections to Jurisdiction, 9 October 2012 [105, 152–153]; *Biwater Gauff (Tanzania) Ltd v. Tanzania*, ICSID Case No. ARB/05/22, Award and Concurring and Dissenting Opinion, 24 July 2008 [587]; *Chevron Corporation and Texaco Petroleum Corporation v. Ecuador*, UNCITRAL, Partial Award on Merits, 30 March 2010 [227]; *CMS Gas Transmission Company v. Argentina*, ICSID Case No. ARB/01/8, Award, 25 April 2005 [270–271, 282]; *Compañía de Aguas del Aconquija SA and Vivendi Universal SA v. Argentina*, ICSID Case No. ARB/97/3, Award, 20 August 2007 [5.2.2., 6.6.2]; *Continental Casualty Company v. Argentina*, ICSID Case No. ARB/03/9, Award, 5 September 2008 [56, 248, 253]; *Duke Energy Electroquil Partners and Electroquil SA v. Ecuador*, ICSID Case No. ARB/04/19, Award, 18 August 2008 [331]; *EDF International SA and ors v. Argentina*, ICSID Case No. ARB/03/23, Final Award, 11 June 2012 [343]; *Electrabel SA v. Hungary*, ICSID Case No. ARB/07/19, Decision on Jurisdiction, Applicable Law and Liability, 30 November 2012 [7.157]; *El Paso Energy International Company v. Argentina*, ICSID Case No. ARB/03/15, Award, 31 October 2011 [329]; *Enron Corporation and Ponderosa Assets, LP v. Argentina*, ICSID Case No. ARB/01/3, Award, 22 May 2007 [253]; *Kardassopoulos v. Georgia and joined case*, ICSID Case Nos. ARB/05/18 and ARB/07/15, Award, 3 March 2010 [409, 417]; *LG&E Energy Corp., LG&E Capital Corp. and LG&E International Inc. v. Argentina*, ICSID Case No. ARB/02/1, Decision on Liability, 3 October 2006 [113]; MCI *Power Group LC and New Turbine Inc v. Ecuador*, ICSID Case No. ARB/03/6, Award, 31 July 2007 [250]; *Metalpar S.A. and Buen Aire S.A. v. Argentina*, ICSID Case No. ARB/03/5, Award on the Merits, 6 June 2008 [117]; *National Grid PLC v. Argentina*, UNCITRAL, Award, 3 November 2008 [161]; *Railroad Development Corporation (RDC) v. Guatemala*, ICSID case No. ARB/07/23, Award, 29 June 2012 [159, 207–211] (referring also to the same position adopted by El Salvador and Honduras); *Rumeli Telekom AS and Telsim Mobil Telekomikasyon Hizmetleri AS v. Kazakhstan*, ICSID Case No. ARB/05/16, Award, 29 July 2008 [611]; *Saluka Investments BV v. Czech Republic*, UNCITRAL, Partial Award, 17 March 2006 [289]; SAUR *International SA v. Argentina*, ICSID Case No. ARB/04/4, Decision on Jurisdiction and Liability, 6 June 2012 [472]; *Sempra Energy International v. Argentina*, ICSID Case No. ARB/02/16, Award, 28 September 2007 [292, 294]; *Suez, Sociedad General de Aguas de Barcelona S.A., and Vivendi Universal S.A. v. Argentina*, ICSID No. ARB/03/19, Decision on Liability, 30 July 2010 [183]; *Ulysseas, Inc v. Ecuador*, UNCITRAL, Final Award, 12 June 2012 [206–207]; *Unglaube and Unglaube v. Costa Rica*, ICSID Case Nos. ARB/08/1 and ARB/09/20, Award, 16 May 2012 [242.].

7 *Mondev International Ltd. v. United States*, ICSID Case No. ARB(AF)/99/2, Award, 2 October 2012 [121]; *Waste Management, Inc. v. Mexico ("Number 2")*, ICSID Case No. ARB(AF)/00/3, Award, 30 April 2004 [91]; *Glamis Gold Ltd v. United States*, UNCITRAL, Award, 14 May 2009 [627]; *Apotex Holdings Inc & Apotex Inc. v. United States*, ICSID Case No. ARB(AF)/12/1,

endorsed by the three NAFTA Parties in their respective pleadings[8] as well as in the Free Trade Commission's 2001 Note of Interpretation.[9] Numerous other awards (outside NAFTA) have also explicitly (or implicitly) acknowledged the customary nature of the MST.[10] The majority of writers have also recognized

---

Award, 25 August 2014 [2.64, 9.15, 9.16, 9.25, 9.27]; *ADF Group Inc. v. United States*, ICSID Case No. ARB(AF)/00/1, Award, 6 January 2003 [179]; *Cargill, Inc. v. Mexico*, ICSID Case No. ARB(AF)/05/02, Award, 18 September 2009 [278]; *Merrill & Ring Forestry L.P. v. Canada*, UNCITRAL, Award, 31 March 2010 [190]; *Eli Lilly and Company v. Canada*, UNCITRAL, Case No. UNCT/14/2, Final Award, 16 March 2017 [223]; *William Ralph Clayton, William Richard Clayton, Douglas Clayton, Daniel Clayton and Bilcon of Delaware, Inc v. Canada*, UNCITRAL PCA Case No. 2009-04, Award on Jurisdiction and Liability, 17 March 2015, [436]; *Windstream Energy LLC v. Canada*, UNCITRAL, Award, 27 September 2016 [350].

8 See, for instance, *ADF* (n 7) [112] (referring to the position of the United States); *Glamis* (n 7) [543] (referring to the position of the United States); *Apotex* (n 7) [2.64]; *Mondev* (n 7) [111].

9 FTC, 'Note of Interpretation of Certain Chapter 11 Provisions', 31 July 2001.

10 See, for instance: *Impregilo S.p.A. v. Argentina*, ICSID Case No. ARB/07/17, Award, 21 June 2001 [285]; *Bayindir* (n 6) [164]; *Biwater Gauff* (n 6) [592]; *CMS* (n 6) [270–271, 282, 284]; *Compañía de Aguas* (n 6) [5.2.2., 6.6.2., 7.4.5., 7.4.6., 7.4.7]; *EDF* (n 6) [343, 999]; *El Paso Energy* (n 6) [329, 335–336]; *Enron* (n 6) [253, 258], see also, Decision on the Application for Annulment of the Argentine Republic, Annulment Committee [302, 304]; *Lauder v. Czech Republic*, UNCITRAL, Final Award, 3 September 2001 [292]; *Lemire v. Ukraine*, ICSID No. ARB/06/18, Decision on Jurisdiction and Liability, 21 January 2010 [250–254], see also, Award, 28 March 2011 [139]; *National Grid* (n 6) [167, 169, 170]; *Occidental Exploration and Production Co v. Ecuador*, LCIA Case No. UN3467, Award, 1 July 2004 [188–192]; *Railroad Development* (n 6) [218]; *Rumeli* (n 6) [611]; *Saluka* (n 6) [289, 291–295]; *SAUR* (n 6) [491]; *Sempra* (n 6) [302]; *Siemens AG v. Argentina*, ICSID No. ARB/02/8, Award, 17 January 2007 [289, 291, 293]; *Suez* (n 6) [184]; *Total SA v. Argentina*, ICSID Case No. ARB/04/1, Decision on Liability, 27 December 2010 [125]; *Ulysseas* (n 6) [206–207, 245]; *Spence International Investments, LLC, Berkowitz, et al v. Costa Rica*, ICSID Case No. Unct/13/2, Interim Award, 30 May 2017 [282]; *Rusoro Mining Ltd. v. Venezuela*, ICSID Case No. ARB(AF)/12/5, Award, 22 August 2016 [513, 520]; *Murphy Exploration & Production Company International v. Ecuador*, PCA Case No. 2012-–16, Partial Final Award, 6 May 2016 [206–208]; *Crystallex International Corporation v. Venezuela*, ICSID Case No. ARB(AF)/11/2, Award, 4 April 2016, [530]; *Quiborax S.A., Non Metallic Minerals S.A. and Allan Fosk Kaplún v. Bolivia*, ICSID Case No. ARB/06/2, Award, 16 September 2015 [290–1]; *ECE Projektmanagement v. The Czech Republic*, UNCITRAL, PCA Case No. 2010–5, Award, 19 September 2013 [4.760]; *Mr. Franck Charles Arif v. Moldova*, ICSID Case No. ARB/11/23, Award, 8 Aril 2013 [529]; *Deutsche Bank AG v. Sri Lanka*, ICSID Case No. ARB/09/2, Award, 31 October 2012 [419]; *Continental Casualty* (n 6) [254]; *Oko Pankki Oyj, VTB Bank (Deutschland) AG and Sampo Bank Plc v. Estonia*, ICSID Case No. ARB/04/6 Award, 19 November 2007 [216]; *Abengoa, S.A. y COFIDES, S.A. v. Mexico*, ICSID Case No. ARB(AF)/09/2, Award, 18 April 2013 [642–3]; *TECO Guatemala*

that the MST is a rule of customary international law;[11] only a few have rejected such a claim.[12]

What is more controversial is determining the actual *content* of the standard. The MST is an *umbrella concept* that in *itself* incorporates different elements. As pointed out by Roth in 1949, 'the international standard is nothing

---

Holdings, LLC v. Guatemala, ICSID Case No. ARB/10/23, Award, 19 December 2013 [455]; *Binder v. Czech Republic*, UNCITRAL, Final Award, 15 July 2001 [484]; *Electrabel* (n 6) [7.158–9]; *OAO Tatneft v. Ukraine*, PCA UNCITRAL, Award on the Merits, 29 July 2014 [392]; *Teinver S.A., Transportes de Cercanías S.A. and Autobuses Urbanos del Sur S.A. v. Argentina*, ICSID Case No. ARB/09/01, Award, 21 July 2017 [666].

11 J.C. Thomas, 'Fair and Equitable Treatment under NAFTA's Investment Chapter; Remarks' (2002) 96 ASIL Proc. 14; Rudolf Dolzer & Margrete Stevens, *Bilateral Investment Treaties* (Martinus Nijhoff 1995) 58; Sir Robert Jenning & Sir Arthur Watts, *Oppenheim's International Law* (9th ed., vol. I, Part 1, Longman 1996) 931; L. Reed, J. Paulsson & N. Blackaby, *A Guide to ICSID Arbitration* (Kluwer Law 2004) 48; Tudor (n 1) 61–62, 67; Andrew Newcombe & Luis Paradell, *Law and Practice of Investment Treaties: Standards of Treatment* (Kluwer 2009) 234; Diehl (n 1) 145; Villanueva (n 1) 63–64; D. Carreau, 'Investissements' in *Répertoire de droit international* (Dalloz 1998) [135]; Hollin Dickerson, 'Minimum Standards' (2013) 9 Max Planck Encyclopedia of Public International Law [1]; Marcela Klein Bronfman, 'Fair and Equitable Treatment: An Evolving Standard' (2006) 10 Max Planck Yrbk. UNL 624; J.C. Thomas, 'Reflections on Article 1105 of NAFTA: History, State Practice and the Influence of Commentators' (2002) 17(1) ICSID Rev. 29ff; J. Roman Picherack, 'The Expanding Scope of the Fair and Equitable Treatment Standard: Have Recent Tribunals Gone Too Far?' (2008) 9(4) J. World Invest. & Trade 265; Graham Mayeda, 'Playing Fair: The Meaning of Fair and Equitable Treatment in Bilateral Investment Treaties' (2007) 41(2) J. World Trade 273–291, 280; Mathias Audit & Mathias Forteau, 'Investment Arbitration without BIT: Toward a Foreign Investment Customary Based Arbitration?' (2012) 29 J. Int. Arb. 640; Paparinskis (n 1) 16, 163; Tarcisio Gazzini, 'The Role of Customary International Law in the Field of Foreign Investment' (2007) 8 J. World Invest. & Trade 699; T. Kill, 'Don't Cross the Streams: Past and Present Overstatement of Customary International Law in Connection with Conventional Fair and Equitable Treatment Obligations' (2008) 106 Michigan LR 853, 856; Jean-Pierre Laviec, *Protection et promotion des investissements, étude de droit international économique* (P.U.F. 1985) 86–88; M.A. Orellana, 'International Law on Investment: The Minimum Standard of Treatment (MST)' (2004) 3 TDM 1–2; Jeswald W. Salacuse, *The Law of Investment Treaties* (Oxford UP 2010) 311; Joel P. Trachtman, 'The Obsolescence of Customary International Law' (2014) SSRN 87–88.

12 M.C. Porterfield, 'An International Common Law of Investor Rights?' (2006) 27 U. Pa. J. Int'l Econ. L. 81–82, 98, 103, 113; M. Sornarajah, *The International Law on Foreign Investment* (2nd ed., Cambridge UP 2004) 64, 92–93 (but, see at 328–329); Stephen Schwebel, 'The United States 2004 Model Bilateral Investment Treaty: An Exercise in the Regressive Development of International Law', in *Global Reflections on International Law, Commerce and Dispute Resolution, Liber Amicorum in honour of Robert Briner* (No. 693, ICC Pub. 2005) 647.

else but a set of rules, correlated to each other and deriving from one particular norm of general international law, namely that the treatment of an alien is regulated by the laws of nations'.[13] Similarly, according to Newcombe *et al.*, the MST 'consists of a series of interconnecting and overlapping elements or standards that apply to both the treatment of foreigners and their property'.[14] A number of NAFTA tribunals have also endorsed the description of the MST as an umbrella concept.[15]

A number of writers have emphasised that the concept of the MST is vague and lacks precise content.[16] For instance, in a recent 2012 report, UNCTAD stated that the minimum standard is 'highly indeterminate, lacks a clearly defined content and requires interpretation'.[17] The report suggested that '[t]he MST is a concept that does not offer ready-made solutions for deciding modern investment disputes; at best, it gives a rough idea of a high threshold that the challenged governmental conduct has to meet for a breach to be established'.[18] As a result, it has been argued that the MST lacks the necessary *normative requirement* (as identified by the International Court of Justice (ICJ) in the *North Sea Continental Shelf* case[19]) in order to be considered as a rule of custom.[20]

An OECD report stated that 'case law points to a number of areas across which the notion of an international minimum standard applies' including 'the administration of justice in cases involving foreign nationals, usually

13 Hans Roth, *The Minimum Standard of International Law Applied to Aliens* (A.W. Sijthoff 1949) 127.

14 Newcombe & Paradell (n 11) 236.

15 See, for instance: *Glamis* (n 7) [618]; *Cargill* (n 7) [268]; *Mobil Investments Canada Inc. & Murphy Oil Corporation v. Canada*, ICSID Case No. ARB(AF)/07/4, Decision on Liability and on Principles of Quantum, 22 May 2012 [135].

16 M. Sornarajah, 'The Fair and Equitable Standard of Treatment: Whose Fairness? Whose Equity?' in Federico Ortino et al. (eds), *Investment Treaty Law: Current Issues II* (BIICL 2007) 172; Sornarajah (n 12) 328; Porterfield (n 12) 80; Gazzini (n 11) 699; Jean d'Aspremont, 'International Customary Investment Law: Story of a Paradox' in T. Gazzini & E. de Brabandere (eds.), *International Investment Law: The Sources of Rights and Obligations* (Martinus Nijhoff 2012) 33.

17 UNCTAD, *Fair and Equitable Treatment*, (2012) UNCTAD Series on Issues in International Investment Agreements II 28, see also 44.

18 Ibid., 46–47.

19 *North Sea Continental Shelf Cases (Federal Republic of Germany v. Denmark / Federal Republic of Germany v. Netherlands)*, [1969] ICJ Rep 42, [72], indicating that a provision must be of a 'fundamentally norm-creating character such as could be regarded as forming the basis of a general rule of law'.

20 d'Aspremont (n 16) 33–34 (see also, at 10–12, 23–24).

linked to the notion of denial of justice', 'the treatment of aliens under detention', full protection and security, and finally, the 'general right of expulsion by the host State' which 'should be the least injurious to the person affected'.[21] A 2012 UNCTAD report came to the same conclusion as that of the OECD.[22] Other writers have defined the content of the minimum standard more broadly.[23] The present author has concluded elsewhere that the MST encompasses (at the very least) an obligation for host States to prevent the denial of justice in the administration of justice, to provide due process, to prevent arbitrary conduct and to provide investors with 'full protection and security'.[24] One of the most controversial questions in the field of investor-State arbitration is whether the FET standard is one of the elements *encompassed* within the larger umbrella concept of the MST or whether it is an autonomous standard. This question is examined below.

1.2 The Historical Foundation of the MST

The historical aspects surrounding the emergence of the MST have already been the subject of substantial scholarship.[25] Moreover, a number of recent

21 OECD, *International Investment Law: A Changing Landscape: A Companion Volume to International Investment Perspectives* (2005) 82. This definition is endorsed by Tudor (n 1) 62.

22 UNCTAD (n 17) 44, referring also to: OECD, *Fair and Equitable Treatment Standard in International Investment Law* (2004) No. 2004/3 Working Papers on International Investment Law. A very similar approach is adopted by Sornarajah (n 12) 172; Sornarajah (n 16) 329.

23 Based on the list mentioned by the tribunal in *Waste Management* (n 7) [98], Newcombe & Paradell (n 11) 238, indicate that a 'number of specific elements of the minimum standard of treatment where state responsibility may arise for mistreatment of foreign investors and investment, including, but not exhaustively: denial of justice, lack of due process, lack of due diligence, and instances of arbitrariness and discrimination'. Paparinskis (n 1) 182, 239, 246–247, 256, argues that denial of justice, arbitrariness and non-discrimination are elements of the MST.

24 Dumberry (n 2) 25–28.

25 *See*, for instance, Edwin Borchard, 'The "Minimum Standard" of the Treatment of Aliens' (1939) 33 ASIL Proc. 55; Edwin Borchard, *The Diplomatic Protection of Citizen Abroad* (Bank Law Publishing Co. 1915); Edwin Borchard, 'The "Minimum Standard" of the Treatment of Aliens' (1940) 38 Mich. L. Rev. 445; Elihu Root, 'The Basis of Protection to Citizens Residing Abroad' (1919) 4 AJIL 521; Clyde Eagleton, *The Responsibility of States in International Law* (New York U. Press 1928) 103; Roth (n 13).

articles[26] and books[27] have also made a significant contribution to the understanding of the concept.

The origin of the MST is grounded in the international law doctrine of State responsibility for injuries to aliens.[28] It is rooted in a due diligence obligation for States to respect the rights of foreigners within their country. Before the twentieth century, there was a prevailing view that individuals conducting business in another State should be subject to the law of that State.[29] This point of view stemmed from the fact that many States, especially in Latin America, strongly opposed other solutions. Several States adopted this position to counter so-called 'gunboat diplomacy' and other types of interferences by Western States in their internal affairs that were often made under the pretext of protecting the interests of their nationals abroad.[30] It is in this context that many States rejected the idea of the existence of any obligation under international law to accord a 'minimum' level of protection to foreigners.[31]

Despite this opposition, a MST gradually emerged in the early twentieth century (which at the time focused almost exclusively on the non-discriminatory aspects of the treatment and on preventing denial of justice[32]).[33] The development of this standard of treatment stemmed from capital-exporting States' concern that many host States of investments lacked the most basic measures of protection for aliens and their property.[34] They argued that all governments were bound under international law to treat foreigners with at

26 See, *inter alia*: Orellana (n 11); Todd Weiler, 'An Historical Analysis of the Function of the Minimum Standard of Treatment in International Investment Law' in Todd Weiler & Freya Baetens (eds), *New Directions in International Economic Law: In Memoriam Thomas Wälde* (Martinus Nijhoff, 2011); Alireza Falsafi, 'The International Minimum Standard of Treatment of Foreign Investors' Property: A Contingent Standard' (2006–2007) 30 Suffolk Transnat'l L. Rev. 317; Hussein Haeri, 'A Tale of Two Standards: 'Fair and Equitable Treatment' and the Minimum Standard in International Law' (2011) 27 Arb. Int'l 31–32.

27 Paparinskis (n 1) 39–83; Weiler (n 1).

28 Dickerson (n 11) [2].

29 Tudor (n 1) 60. This period is examined in detail in: Weiler (n 26) 337 ff.

30 Weiler (n 26) 345, providing a number of examples of such interventions and referring to 'no fewer than one hundred instances of "protection by force" between 1813 and 1927 by the United States alone, including two dozen in the 20th century'.

31 S. Schill, *The Multilateralization of International Investment Law* (Cambridge UP 2009) 26–27.

32 Paparinskis (n 1) 64.

33 Weiler (n 26) 351.

34 Orellana (n 11) 1.

least a minimum standard of protection[35] because the existing standard in many countries was considered too low.[36] The reasons for establishing such a standard were explained by US Secretary of State, Mr. Elihu Root, in an article published in 1910[37] and were reiterated some 90 years later by the NAFTA *S.D. Myers* tribunal explaining that the 'minimum standard' is a floor below which treatment of foreign investors must not fall'.[38] The *Glamis* Tribunal would subsequently explained that the standard is 'meant to serve as a floor, an absolute bottom, below which conduct is not accepted by the international community', adding that the standard 'cannot vary between nations as thus the protection afforded would have no minimum'.[39]

International jurisprudence slowly developed the concept of a minimum standard of protection.[40] While a number of cases have had a significant impact on the emergence of this standard,[41] the best known is certainly the *Neer* case in 1926. This case was decided by the US-Mexico Claims Commission, which was established in the 1920s to adjudicate claims arising out of widespread unrest in Mexico.[42] The Commission held that the 'propriety of governmental acts should be put to the test of international standards' and that 'the treatment of an alien, in order to constitute an international delinquency,

35 C. Schreuer & R. Dolzer, *Principles of International Investment Law* (Oxford UP 2008) 12–13.

36 Salacuse (n 11) 47; Thomas (n 11) 26.

37 Root (n 25) 521: 'Each country is bound to give to the nationals of another country in its territory the benefit of the same laws, the same administration, the same protection, and the same redress for injury which it gives to its own citizens, and neither more nor less: *provided the protection which the country gives to its own citizens conforms to the established standard of civilization.* There is [however] a standard of justice very simple, very fundamental, and of such general acceptance by all civilized countries as to form a part of the international law of the world. The ... system of law and administration shall conform to this general standard. If any country's system of law and administration does not conform to that standard, although the people of the country may be content to live under it, no other country can be compelled to accept it as furnishing a satisfactory measure of treatment of its citizens' (emphasis added). On this question, see Paparinskis (n 1) 39–46.

38 *S.D. Myers Inc. v. Canada*, UNCITRAL, First Partial Award, 13 November 2000 [259].

39 *Glamis* (n 7) [615].

40 M. Kinnear, A. Biorklund & J.F.G. Hannaford, *Investment Disputes under NAFTA: An Annotated Guide to NAFTA Chapter 11* (Kluwer Law 2006), section on Art. 1105, at 11–12; Orellana (n 11) 2.

41 See, *inter alia: Roberts v. Mexico*, Award, 2 November 1926, 4 UNRIAA 77; *Chevreau v. United Kingdom*, Award, 9 June 1931, 2 UNRIAA 1113; *George W. Hopkins v. Mexico*, Award, 31 March 1926, 4 UNRIAA 41, 50.

42 *USA (LF Neer) v. Mexico*, Award, 15 October 1926, 4 UNRIAA 60.

should amount to an outrage, to bad faith, to willful neglect of duty, or to an insufficiency of governmental action so far short of international standards that every reasonable and impartial man would readily recognize its insufficiency.'[43]

As noted by one writer, 'the Commission attempted to define the international standard by means of analogy, deriving criteria of procedural outrage from the better-established rules of denial of justice and then applying these more generally'.[44] Although the *Neer* case did not used the expression MST, it has had considerable influence on the emergence of the concept.[45] This conclusion has recently been contested by a number of tribunals[46] and several writers who have argued that little weight should be accorded to a three-page award that only makes a general statement and is not substantiated by State practice.[47] In the recent *Railroad Development Corporation* case, the Tribunal

43 Ibid., 61–62.

44 Paparinskis (n 1) 64.

45 Roth (n 13) 95. The case is discussed in detail in: Thomas (n 11) 29ff; Paparinskis (n 1) 48–54.

46 *Mondev* (n 7) [115]: 'The Tribunal would observe, however, that the *Neer* case, and other similar cases which were cited, concerned not the treatment of foreign investment as such but the physical security of the alien. Moreover the specific issue in *Neer* was that of Mexico's responsibility for failure to carry out an effective police investigation into the killing of a United States citizen by a number of armed men who were not even alleged to be acting under the control or at the instigation of Mexico. In general, the State is not responsible for the acts of private parties, and only in special circumstances will it become internationally responsible for a failure in the conduct of the subsequent investigation. Thus there is insufficient cause for assuming that provisions of bilateral investment treaties, and of NAFTA, while incorporating the *Neer* principle in respect of the duty of protection against acts of private parties affecting the physical security of aliens present on the territory of the State, are confined to the *Neer* standard of outrageous treatment where the issue is the treatment of foreign investment by the State itself'. Another example is *Merrill & Ring* (n 7) [197] (noting that the *Neer* and others cases were 'dealing with situations concerning due process of law, denial of justice and physical mistreatment, and only marginally with matters relating to business, trade or investments'), [204] ('No general rule of customary international law can thus be found which applies the *Neer* standard, beyond the strict confines of personal safety, denial of justice and due process'). More recently, the NAFTA Tribunal in *Windstream* (n 7) [352] also concluded that the *Neer* decision did not 'deal with the treatment of foreign investors, and consequently the factual circumstances of the [*Neer*] case are in any event not directly relevant here'.

47 Stephen M. Schwebel, 'Is Neer far from Fair and Equitable?' (2011) 27(4) Arb. Int'l 555–561; Jan Paulsson, 'Neer-lv Misled?' Miami Law Research Paper 247 (see also: J. Paulsson & G. Petrochilos, 'Neer-ly Misled?' (2007) 22(2) ICSID Rev. 242–257). See also: Newcombe & Paradell (n 11) 237; Tudor (n 1) 64; Kläger (n 1) 53.

also stated that the Commission 'did not formulate the minimum standard of treatment after an analysis of State practice' and further noted that it was 'ironic that the decision considered reflecting the expression of the minimum standard of treatment in customary international law is based on the opinions of commentators and, on its own admission, went further than their views without an analysis of State practice followed because of a sense of obligation'.[48] Others have rightly highlighted the fact that the case does not involve any issue related to the protection of investments per se;[49] therefore arguing that the award would only be relevant for 'cases of failure to arrest and punish private actors of crimes against aliens'.[50]

It is suffice to conclude (in the context of the present book[51]) that the *Neer* case offers little value when determining the *actual* content of the MST in contemporary international investment law due to the fact that the standard has evolved substantially since the 1920s. This position has been adopted by several tribunals[52] as well as by many scholars.[53] Other tribunals[54] have come to the same conclusion regarding the *Roberts* case, which was decided by the US-Mexico General Claims Commission in 1926 and involved a US citizen who had been imprisoned in Mexico in what he held to be inhumane conditions.[55] The

48 *Railroad* (n 6) [216]. The Tribunal also added that 'by the strict standards of proof of customary international law applied in *Glamis Gold*, *Neer* would fail to prove its famous statement (...) to be an expression of customary international law'.

49 R. Jennings, 'General Course on Principles of International Law', 121 Rec. des cours (1967-II) 487; Laviec (n 11) 88.

50 Paulsson (n 47) 247. See also: Schwebel (n 47).

51 See, the analysis in Dumberry (n 2) 16–19.

52 *ADF* (n 7) [181]; *Mondev* (n 7) [116, 117]; *Loewen Group, Inc. and Raymond L. Loewen v. United States*, ICSID Case No. ARB(AF)/98/3, Award on Merits, 26 June 2003 [132]; *Philip Morris Brands Sàrl, Philip Morris Products S.A. and Abal Hermanos S.A. v. Uruguay*, ICSID Case No. ARB/10/7, Award, 8 July 2016 [319]; *Crystallex* (n 10) [534]; *Gold Reserve Inc. v. Venezuela*, ICSID Case No. ARB(AF)/09/1, Award, 22 September 2014 [567]; *Windstream* (n 7) [352]; *Bilcon* (n 7) [434–5]; *Mesa Power Group, LLC v. Canada*, UNCITRAL PCA Case No. 2012–17, Award, 24 March 2016 [496–501].

53 Newcombe & Paradell (n 11) 237; Tudor (n 1) 64; Kläger (n 1) 53; Paulsson (n 47) 257. For Paparinskis (n 1) 216, the *Neer* case 'operates as the default rule', to be 'replaced by more specific and detailed rules on the Issue when they exist or are developed'.

54 *Rusoro* (n 10) [517–519]; *OI European Group B.V. v. Venezuela*, ICSID Case No. ARB/11/25, Award, 10 March 2015 [489].

55 *Roberts* (n 41).

Commission defined the minimum treatment as that required 'in accordance with ordinary standards of civilization'.[56]

The question of whether or not any customary rule in the field of investment arbitration had firmly crystallized after the Second World War has solicited plenty of controversy.[57] However, it is safe to say that the MST was an established rule of custom at the time.[58] One writer has, however, recently argued that in the period before the Second World War the MST which emerged was originally based from the concept of 'general principles recognized by civilized nations' (which are found in the *domestic laws* of States), and therefore *not* based on customary international law.[59]

The next section will examine a number of dramatic developments that occurred in the decades following the Second World War.

1.3 The Challenge to Existing Customary Rules, including the MST, Led by Newly Independent States in the 1960s and 1970s

In the 1960s and 1970s, a group of States revived the opposition towards the existence of any custom rules in the field of investment law. This era was

---

56 Id.: 'Facts with respect to equality of treatment of aliens and nationals may be important in determining the merits of a complaint of mistreatment of an alien. But such equality is not the ultimate test of the propriety of the acts of authorities in the light of international law. That test is, broadly speaking, whether aliens are treated in accordance with ordinary standards of civilization. We do not hesitate to say that the treatment of Roberts was such as to warrant an indemnity on the ground of cruel and inhumane imprisonment'. According to *Lemire* (n 10) [249]: 'Roberts is understood to stand for the propositions that a certain treatment may give rise to international responsibility notwithstanding that it affects citizens and aliens alike, and that administrative and legislative actions may amount to a violation of the customary minimum treatment even if the State did not act in bad faith or with willful neglect of duty'.

57 Patrick Juillard, 'L'évolution des sources du droit des investissements', (1994) 250 Rec. des Cours 76.

58 This is indeed the position taken by these writers in the 1950s: Robert R. Wilson, *The International Law Standard in Treaties of the United States* (Harvard UP 1953) 103–104; G. Schwarzenberger, *International Law* (vol. 1, 3rd ed. Stevens & Sons 1957) 206–207. See also: Paparinskis (n 1) 64–67, 83 ff.

59 Andrew C. Blandford, 'The History of Fair and Equitable Treatment before the Second World War', (2017) 32(2) ICSID Rev. 294ff, referring, *inter alia*, to the famous 1910 speech by former US Secretary of State Elihu Root and to the early work of Borchard. On the *Neer* case, he noted that: 'Today, the Neer standard is often cited as a classic formulation of the minimum standard under customary international law. However, the Neer Commission did not purport to articulate customary international law. It derived the standard from the general principles of justice and equity'.

fundamentally marked by the arrival on the international scene of a growing number of 'Newly Independent States' who were emerging from colonialism in both Asia and Africa. These new States openly contested the *legitimacy* of existing customary international law.[60] They demanded a revision of the 'outdated' rules that did not take into account the fundamental changes that had occurred in the international community since the end of the colonisation period.[61] According to Abi-Saab, these States '[did] not easily forget that the same body of international law that they [were] now asked to abide by, sanctioned their previous subjugation and exploitation and stood as a bar to their emancipation'.[62]

Specifically, these States rejected the obligation of having to provide any minimum standard of protection to foreign investors under customary international law.[63] They insisted that 'States were bound to accord the foreign investor only national treatment, only what their domestic law provided'.[64] They also contested the existence of any international law norms requiring compensation for expropriated foreign properties and supported a less stringent compensation requirement than the Hull formula.[65] At the time, developing States took the debate to the United Nations General Assembly where they represented the majority of States.[66] They used their status within the international body to advance their interests by way of resolutions and declarations,[67] which included Resolution 3171 adopted in 1973[68] and the 1974 *Charter of Economic Rights and Duties of States*.[69]

60 Andrew T. Guzman, 'Why LDCs Sign Treaties That Hurt Them: Explaining the Popularity of Bilateral Investment Treaties' (1998) 38(4) Va.J.Int'l L. 64; Juillard (n 57) 76.

61 Georges Abi-Saab, 'The Newly Independent States and the Rules of International Law: An Outline' (1962) 8 Howard L.J. 118.

62 Ibid., 100. See also: S.N. Guha-Roy, 'Is the Law of Responsibility of States for Injuries to Aliens A Part of Universal International Law?' (1961) 55 AJIL 866.

63 Sornarajah (n 12) 140ff; OECD (n 22) 82. See, for instance: 'Report of the Fourth Session of the Asian African Legal Consultative Committee' (1961) 2 ILC YB 78, 82–84.

64 Schwebel (n 12) 3.

65 Guzman (n 60) 647; UNCTAD, *Bilateral Investment Treaties 1995–2006: Trends in Investment Rulemaking* (2007) 48.

66 Juillard (n 57) 84ff.

67 M. Byers, *Custom, Power and the Power of Rules: International Relations and Customary International Law* (Cambridge UP 1999) 41.

68 UNGA Res 3171 (1974) GAOR, 28th Session Supp. 30, 52, U.N. Doc. A/9030 in (1974) 13 ILM 238.

69 UNGA Res 3281 (1974) U.N. GAOR, 29th Session Supp 31, 50–55, U.N. Doc. A/9631 in (1975) 14 ILM 251.

What has been the impact of said contestation on custom? One thing is clear: considering the opposition between developed and developing States, the *Charter of Economic Rights and Duties of States* could hardly be considered as a reflection of existing international law at the time.[70] Another question raised is whether or not the effect of the attack by new States had been to *destroy* the few rules of custom that existed after the Second World War. A number of writers believe this was the case.[71] Without specifically taking a position on the impact that the contestation may have had on custom, the ICJ in the famous *Barcelona Traction* case of 1970 simply noted that *no rule* of customary international law existed in the field of international investment law:

> Considering the important developments of the last half-century, the growth of foreign investments and the expansion of international activities of corporations, in particular of holding companies, which are often multinational, and considering the way in which the economic interests of states have proliferated, it may at first sight appear surprising that the evolution of the law has not gone further and that no generally accepted rules in the matter have crystallized on the international plane.[72]

The more established position, as mentioned above, is that some customary rules *already existed* at the time when developing States started opposing them. Thus, while contested by many States, it remains that the MST had long been established as a basic rule of custom.[73] In the 1990 *ELSI* case, the ICJ indeed

70 Stephen M. Schwebel, 'Investor-State Disputes and the Development of International Law: The Influence of Bilateral Investment Treaties on Customary International Law' (2004) 98 ASIL Proceedings 28; Schwebel (n 12) 1; C. Brower & Tepe, 'Charter of Economic Rights and Duties of States-A Reflection or Rejection of International Law?' (1975) 9 Int'l Law 295; D. Carreau & P. Juillard, *Droit international économique* (LGDJ 1998) 464; Salacuse (n 11) 75.

71 Carreau & Juillard, ibid., 464–5; Sornarajah (n 12) 19–20, 89–93, 213; A. Akinsanya, 'International Protection of Direct Foreign Investments in the Third World' (1987) 36 ICLQ 58; Abdullah Al Faruque, 'Creating Customary International Law Through Bilateral Investment Treaties: A Critical Appraisal' (2004) 44 Indian JIL 312–313; d'Aspremont (n 16) 14.

72 *Barcelona Traction, Light and Power Co., Ltd. (Belgium v. Spain)*, [1970] ICJ Rep 3 [46–47].

73 See, Dumberry (n 3) 96; Paparinskis (n 1) 83 ff; Jose E. Alvarez, 'Bit on Custom' (2009–2010) 42 NYU J. Int'l L. & Pol. 39; José E. Alvarez, 'The Public International Law Regime Governing International Investment' (2009) 344 Rec. des cours 292. But see, Schwebel (n 12) 4 for whom 'There was, and is, no agreement within the international community

referred explicitly to the existence of a 'minimum international standard'.[74] In fact, while it seems that the MST survived the assault by developing States, it did not do so without some casualties. Thus, as noted by one writer, the strong contestation of a large segment of States has 'served to undermine the solidity of the traditional international legal framework for foreign investment'.[75] Thus, while developed States held the view that customary rules existed, they also acknowledged that their effectiveness was limited as a result of the vehement opposition of a large number of States.[76] In fact, both developed and developing States perceived these rules as ineffective in providing basic legal protection to foreign investors.[77] As discussed further below, it is in this historical context that in the 1990s States began signing numerous BITs providing clearer rules on investment protection.

1.4 The New Phenomenon of 'Treatification' in the 1990s

This new phenomenon of numerous States starting to sign BITs in the early 1990s has been referred to as 'treatification'. This was a period marked by globalisation whereby private foreign investments were (almost) universally deemed by States as essential tools for their economic development.[78] At the time, a newly found consensus emerged regarding the necessity to offer

---

on the content of 'the customary international law minimum standard of treatment of aliens', or even on whether such a minimum standard existed or exists'.

74 *Sicula S.p.A. (ELSI) (US v. Italy)* (Judgment) [1989], ICJ Rep 115 [111] ('The primary standard laid down by Article V is "the full protection and security required by international law", in short the "protection and security" must conform to the minimum international standard').

75 Salacuse (n 11) 45–46, 75; Al Faruque (n 71) 294–295.

76 The member States of the OECD certainly believed at the time that these customary rules existed. Thus, the OECD, *Draft Convention on the Protection of Foreign Property*, (1967) 7 ILM 117, Article 1 cmt., explicitly used the expression 'minimum standard which forms part of customary international law'. It should be noted that the OECD used a different expression ('general principles of international law') in its 1984 study: OECD Committee on International Investment and Multinational Enterprise, *Inter-Governmental Agreements Relating to Investment in Developing Countries*, Doc. No. 84/14, 27 May 1984, at 12, [36]. On this question, see OECD (n 22) 97.

77 d'Aspremont (n 16) 16; Salacuse (n 11) 76. See also: Jeswald W. Salacuse, *The Three Laws of International Investment National, Contractual, and International Frameworks for Foreign Capital* (Oxford UP 2013) 329–330.

78 Thus, the 1992 *World Bank Guidelines* on the Treatment of Foreign Direct Investment explained in its preamble that it 'recognizes' that 'a greater flow of foreign direct investment brings substantial benefits to bear on the world economy and on the economies of developing countries in particular'.

better legal protection to foreign investments in order to accelerate such development. Yet, there was still great uncertainty surrounding the types of legal protections that existed for foreign investors under custom. Not surprisingly, efforts by the OECD to negotiate a comprehensive Multilateral Agreement on Investment (MAI) in 1995 were unsuccessful.[79] As explained by two scholars, it is due to the fact that 'customary law was deemed be too amorphous and not be able to provide sufficient guidance and protection' to foreign investors that capital-exporting and developing States started frenetically concluding *ad hoc* BITs.[80] The same conclusion is reached by many writers,[81] including Kläger:

> Many states felt that an international minimum standard – whatever concrete contours it had – existed, but also that it had been challenged every now and again. Due to the failure to establish a multilateral framework for foreign investments, states pursued the reaffirmation and clarification of the legal status of foreign investments through the conclusion of bilateral treaties. In this way, states tried to overcome the uncertainty pertaining to the customary law in this field and to establish a firmer set of rules that applied at least *inter partes*.[82]

According to Schreuer and Dolzer, as a result of the new climate of international economic relations of the 1990s, 'the fight of previous decades against customary rules protecting foreign investment had abruptly become anachronistic and obsolete'.[83] Consequently, by the 1990s, 'the tide had turned' and developing States were no longer opposed to the application of a minimum

---

79 For a draft text, see *Multilateral Agreement on Investment*, Draft Consolidated Text, DAFFE/MAI(98)7/REV1 (22 April 1998).

80 R. Dolzer & A. von Walter, 'Fair and Equitable Treatment – Lines of Jurisprudence on Customary Law' in F. Ortino (ed), *Investment Treaty Law, Current Issues II* (2007) 99.

81 Orellana (n 11) 3; Laviec (n 11) 87–88; Campbell McLachlan, 'Investment Treaties and General International Law' (2008) 57 ICLQ 365; Jeswald W. Salacuse, 'BIT by BIT: The Growth of Bilateral Investment Treaties and Their Impact on Foreign Investment in Developing Countries' (1990) 24 Int'l L. 659; B. Kishoiyan, 'The Utility of Bilateral Investment Treaties in the Formulation of Customary International Law' (1993) 14(2) Northwestern J. Int'l L. 332, 372; Al Faruque (n 71) 293; d'Aspremont (n 16) 16–18.

82 Kläger (n 1) 263–4. See also: Jeswald W. Salacuse, 'Towards a Global Treaty on Foreign Investment: the Search for a Grand Bargain' in N. Horn and S. Kröll (eds), *Arbitrating Foreign Investment Disputes: Procedural and Substantive Legal Aspects* (2004) 58; Salacuse (n 11) 77; C. McLachlan, L. Shore & M. Weiniger, *International Investment Arbitration: Substantive Principles* (Oxford UP 2007) 17.

83 Schreuer & Dolzer (n 35) 16.

standard of protection under custom. Instead, they granted 'more protection to foreign investment than traditional customary law did, now on the basis of treaties negotiated to attract additional foreign investment'.[84]

It is now estimated that 3,268 international investment agreements ('IIAs') provide investors with investment protection,[85] including 2,923 BITs.[86] As a result of these developments, the number of arbitration cases between investors and States is booming. The most recent UNCTAD Report mentions a total of 767 known cases.[87]

The next section examines how this new phenomenon of 'treatification' was marked by the emergence of the FET standard and the decline of the MST as a source of investment protection for foreign investors.

2 *The Emergence of the FET Standard in Investment Treaties and Its Interaction with the MST*

I will first examine the early appearance of the FET standard in multilateral instruments after the Second World War and the fact that it is now contained in the overwhelming majority of BITs (Section 2.1.). The following sections examine the question of the interaction between the FET standard and the MST. The central question analysed is why States started referring to the FET standard instead of the MST in their investment treaties? (Section 2.2.). I will then address the implication of the answer to this question. I will argue that FET should be considered as a standard independent from the MST (except in some specific situations) (Section 2.3.).

2.1 Early Appearance of the Standard in Multilateral Instruments and Current Overwhelming Presence in BITs

The history of the emergence of the FET clause has previously been examined in detail by several authors.[88] For the purposes of this book, it suffices to

---

84 Ibid., see also: Schwebel (n 12) 28.

85 UNCTAD, *Recent Trends, in IIAs and ISDS*, (2015) 1 IIA Issues Note 2. See also: World Bank, *World Investment Report* (2014) xxiii.

86 UNCTAD, ibid., 2.

87 UNCTAD, *Investor–State Dispute Settlement: Review of Developments in 2016*, ILA Issue Notes No. 1, 2017, 1.

88 See *inter alia*: Stephen Vasciannie, 'The Fair and Equitable Treatment Standard in International Investment Law and Practice' (1999) 70 British YIL 99; Thomas (n 11); Kinnear et al. (n 40) 23; UNCTAD, *Fair and Equitable Treatment*, UNCTAD Series on Issues in International Investment Agreements (1999); UNCTAD (n 17) 5ff; Haeri (n 26) 83ff; Blandford (n 59) 287–303. See also, more recently: Mona Pinchis-Paulsen, 'The Life and Death (and Re-Birth) of "Fair and" "Equitable Treatment:" A Historical Examination of

simply highlight some of the most salient features of these important historical developments.

The first reference to 'equitable treatment' can be found at Article 23(e) of the League of Nations Covenant, which commits its member States 'to secure and maintain … equitable treatment for the commerce of all Members of the League'.[89] The 1948 *Havana Charter for an International Trade Organization* is generally considered as the first legal instrument that makes reference to the FET standard.[90] The Havana Charter never came into force. At the same time, the Organization of American States adopted the *Economic Agreement of Bogotá* in 1948, which mentioned at Article 22 that 'foreign capital shall receive equitable treatment'.[91] The document was, however, never ratified.[92] Ten years later in 1959, a group of European businesspersons and lawyers under the leadership of Mr. Hermann Abs and Lord Shawcross drafted the Abs-Shawcross *Draft Convention on Investments Abroad.* The document specifically offered protection in terms of 'fair and equitable treatment' to foreigner's property.[93] The clause offered wide protection and covered 'the most constant protection and security' and forbade discrimination against a foreigner's property.

Twentieth Century International Trade and Investment Law Treaty-Making and Political Decision-Making' (Ph.D. Thesis, University of London (King's College), 2017).

89 See the analysis of Kill (n 11) 869ff. A detailed account of this provision can be found in: Mona Pinchis, 'The Ancestry of 'Equitable Treatment' in Trade: Lessons from the League of Nations during the Inter-War Period', (2014) 15 J. World Invest. & Trade, 13–72.

90 Havana Charter for an International Trade Organization, Mar. 24, 1948, Art. 11(2), in: U.N. Conference on Trade & Employment, Final Act and Related Documents 8–9, U.N. Doc. E/Conf. 2/78, U.N. Sales No. 1948.II.D.4 (1948). Although the Havana Charter focused on trade issues, it also contained a number of provisions related to investments including a reference that a future organization would be authorized to 'make recommendations for and promote bilateral or multilateral agreements on measure designed … to assure just and equitable treatment for the enterprise …'. See: Thomas (n 11) 40ff; Kill (n 11) 871–873. A number of other initiatives are discussed in: Weiler (n 26) 358ff.

91 Organization of American States, Economic Agreement of Bogotá, Art. 22, May 1948, L. Treaty Ser. No. 25, OAS Doc. No. OEA/Ser.A/4 (SEPF). The full provision reads as follows: '[f]oreign capital shall receive equitable treatment. The States therefore agree not to take unjustified, unreasonable or discriminatory measures that would impair the legally acquired rights or interests of nationals of other countries in the enterprises, capital, skills, arts or technology they have supplied'.

92 Kill (n 11) 873.

93 Art. 1. Hermann Abs & Hartley Shawcross, 'The Proposed Convention to Protect Private Foreign Investment: A Round Table: Comment on the Draft Convention by its Authors', (1960) 9 JPL 115–132.

In 1967, the OECD developed a convention to protect private property: the *Draft Convention on the Protection of Foreign Property* (hereinafter 'Draft Convention').[94] It provides that 'each party shall at all times ensure FET to the property of the nationals of the other parties'.[95] One of the reasons why the Draft Convention included such a reference to FET may be because several OECD members had, at the time, already started to adopt the FET clause in their respective BITs (a point discussed below).[96] Although the Draft Convention was never opened for signature, its importance should not be underestimated since it 'represented the collective view and dominant trend of OECD countries on investment issues'.[97] The Draft Convention also provided OECD member States with guidelines that were subsequently used by them as a model to draft their own BITs.[98] In fact, it has been rightly observed that the many textual similarities between the different treaty models used by developed OECD member States as a basis for treaty negotiation with developing countries, has led to a greater uniformity in BIT language.[99] Thus, the origin of the FET clause that is now commonly found in modern BITs can (at least in part) be traced to this 1967 OECD Draft Convention.[100]

On the bilateral level, the first group of BITs that mentioned the FET were those concluded by European States (including Germany and Switzerland) in the early 1960s.[101] By the 1970s, FET was specifically mentioned in most BITs between capital-exporting and capital-importing countries.[102] According to some estimates, the standard was mentioned in over 300 BITs between the 1960s and 1990s.[103]

From the 1990s and onwards, States have included the FET standard in an overwhelming majority of BITs.[104] A detailed analysis conducted in the early 1990s of 335 BITs shows that only 28 BITs did not include a reference to FET.[105]

94 OECD (n 76).
95 Article 1(a).
96 K.J. Vandevelde, *Bilateral Investment Treaties: History, Policy and Interpretation*, (Oxford UP 2010) 199.
97 OECD (n 76) 2ff.
98 Ibid.; Tudor (n 1) 19; Bronfman (n 11) 161.
99 K.J. Vandevelde, 'The Political Economy of a Bilateral Investment Treaty', (1988) 92 AJIL, 621, 628; Vasciannie (n 88) 113.
100 Vasciannie, ibid., 113.
101 Vandevelde (n 96) 196.
102 UNCTAD (n 17) 8–9; OECD (n 22) 78.
103 M. Khalil, *Treatment of Foreign Investment in BITs*, 8 ICSID Rev, 355 (1992).
104 Tudor (n 1) 23.
105 Khalil (n 103) 351–355.

This is confirmed by Tudor's book published in 2008 examining 365 BITs with only 19 of them not containing a reference to FET.[106] The present author has examined elsewhere all 1,964 BITs that were available on the UNCTAD website[107] at the time (February 2014) and found that only 50 of them did not include an FET clause at all, while 25 others only referred to the FET in their preamble.[108] Thus, less than 5% of the BITs examined do not include any formal and binding FET obligation for the host State of investments.

While the vast majority of BITs include an FET clause, there nevertheless remains a considerable degree of variation in the actual content of the clause. These variations can be summarized as follows:[109]

- Reference to the FET solely in a treaty preamble which therefore does not impose any binding obligations on the host State.
- Autonomous and unqualified reference to the FET.
- Reference to the FET in combination with other standards of protection (such as national treatment and the most-favored-nations clause).
- Reference to the FET with an additional specification that this treatment prohibits arbitrary and discretionary measures.
- Reference to the FET combined with a reference to international law.
- Reference to the FET combined with a reference to customary international law.

As further discussed below, the most significant distinction is between, on the one hand, 'stand-alone' clauses containing an 'unqualified' reference to the obligation to accord a FET, and, on the other hand, clauses referring to a FET obligation linked to 'international law'. Importantly, only a few treaties

---

106 Tudor (n 1) 23.

107 http://investmentpolicyhub.unctad.org/IIA. I have examined BITs available in a number of languages including English, French, Spanish, etc, but not those in Arabic or Russian.

108 P. Dumberry, 'Has the Fair and Equitable Treatment Standard become a Rule of Customary international Law?' (2016) 8(1) J. Int. Disp. Settl. 155–178.

109 The present typology is based on the work of Tudor (n 1) 22ff; Kläger (n 1) 9ff.; Diehl (n 1) 129ff. UNCTAD (n 17) xiii, identifies four different approaches: '(a) Unqualified obligation to accord fair and equitable treatment; (b) FET obligation linked to international law; (c) FET obligation linked to the minimum standard of treatment of aliens under customary international law; (d) FET obligation with additional substantive content such as denial of justice'.

contain FET clauses specifically referring to the MST, including notably the NAFTA and the CAFTA-DR (a point discussed further below).[110]

This next Chapter will examine the controversial question as to why States started referring to the FET standard instead of the MST in their investment treaties.

2.2 Why Did States Start Referring to the FET Standard instead of the MST in Their Investment Treaties?

One of the most controversial questions discussed in scholarship is why States first began including the term FET in their BITs throughout the 1960s and 1970s, and why they have continued to do so (almost) uniformly thereafter in the 1990s.[111]

According to one view, Western States incorporated the concept of FET in their BITs to simply reflect the MST that existed under international law.[112] This approach has been endorsed by a number of writers.[113] These writers

110 One rare older example of such a clause is found in a Protocol to the BIT between the Netherlands and Venezuela, which was signed on the same day as the BIT, and providing (at Ad Article 3(1)): 'The Contracting Parties agree that the treatment of investments shall be considered to be fair and equitable as mentioned in Article 3, paragraph 1, if it conforms to the treatment accorded to investments of their own nationals, or to investments of nationals of any third State, whichever is more favorable to the national concerned, as well as to the *minimum standard for the treatment of foreign nationals under international law*'). The provision is examined in: *ConocoPhillips Petrozuata B.V., ConocoPhillips Hamaca B.V. and ConocoPhillips Gulf of Paria B.V. v. Venezuela*, ICSID Case No. ARB/07/30, Decision on Jurisdiction and Merits, 3 September 2013 [291ff].

111 See, discussion in Dumberry (n 2) 31–35.

112 See, analysis in Newcombe & Paradell (n 11) 268; Thomas (n 11) 44, 47; Carreau & Julliard (n 70) 454.

113 See, for instance: Picherack (n 11) 264 ('When the language of fair and equitable treatment first began to emerge in draft multilateral instruments and investment agreements in the 1950s and 1960s, it was likely then intended to serve as a reference to the minimum standard of treatment existing in international law.... The desire to set down a fair and equitable treatment provision in the text of multilateral instruments and investment agreements could be seen as an attempt at the time to solidify the minimum international standard in the face of the Calvo doctrine and many developing countries' assertions which denied the existence of a minimum standard of treatment in customary international law separate from a national treatment standard'); Paparinskis (n 1) 160–163 ('If one takes together the pre- and post-Second World War materials pre-dating investment arbitrations, it seems permissible to conclude that the ordinary meaning of fair and equitable treatment was a reference to customary minimum standard, in particular regarding administration of justice'); S. Montt, *State Liability in Investment Treaty*

typically refer to the 1967 OECD Draft Convention[114] as representative of the position of developed States at the time on matters of protection of foreign investments.[115] This is because the OECD's Commentary to the 1967 Draft Convention indicated that the concept of FET flowed from the 'well established general principle of international law that a State is bound to respect and protect the property of nationals of other States'.[116] The Drafting Committee also added that the phrase FET refers to 'the standard set by international law for the treatment due by each State with regard to the property of foreign nationals' and that 'the standard required conforms in effect to the minimum standard which forms part of customary international law'.[117] The same position was also taken by OECD member States in 1984.[118] This position is also confirmed by the practice of some Western States.[119] This narrative has, however, been subject to dissent by many scholars.[120] While it is possible that the OECD commentary reflected what their member States (all developed States) *themselves* viewed as what was customary international law at the time, they were

Arbitration (Hart Publ. 2009) 69 ('If the historical background is to be taken seriously, then the FET standard, when first used, could not have meant anything higher than IMS. At a time when the opposing North-South legal camps were, respectively, IMS and national treatment, the FET standard could not have referred to either an autonomous standard or to a higher standard than those minima'); Blandford (n 59) 302 ('at the time when the United States introduced FET provisions to post-war treaty negotiations, 'just and equitable treatment' was already a term of art for what we now call the minimum standard').

114 OECD (n 76).

115 Vasciannie (n 88) 112–113; UNCTAD (n 17) 8; OECD (n 22) 4.

116 OECD (n 76) 119.

117 Ibid.

118 Thomas (n 11) 48 referring to: OECD Committee (n 76) 12 [36] ('[a]ccording to all Member countries which have commented on this point, fair and equitable treatment introduced a substantive legal standard referring to general principles of international law even if this is not explicitly stated').

119 See, examples examined by Newcombe & Paradell (n 11) 268 (referring to US, UK, Swiss and Canadian treaty practice); Thomas (n 11) 48–51; Paparinskis (n 1) 162 ('pleadings in the ICJ (…) show that such States as Belgium, Spain, the UK, and the US used the language of fair and equitable treatment to refer to the customary of law administration of justice'). On Swiss practice, see: Statement of the Swiss Department of External Affairs (Mémoire, JAAC 1979, fasc. 43/IV, no. 113) in: L. Caflisch, 'La pratique suisse en matière de droit international public', (1980) 36 ASDI 178 ('On se réfère ainsi au principe classique du droit des gens selon lequel les États doivent mettre les étrangers se trouvant sur leur territoire et leurs biens au bénéfice du "standard minimum" international, c'est-à-dire leur accorder un minimum de droits personnels, procéduraux et économiques"').

120 Kill (n 11) 876–877; Bronfman (n 11) 615.

certainly not representative of what developing States believed was their legal obligations in the 1960s.[121]

As explained by two scholars, the use of a 'different and more politically neutral term [FET] might be explained by the historical political sensitivities regarding the minimum standard of treatment', which was 'historically viewed with suspicion because of the legacy of gun-boat diplomacy and imperialism'.[122] This is also the position endorsed by Judge Nikken in his separate opinion in the *AWG Group v. Argentina* case.[123] For these writers, the concept of the FET 'may simply have been viewed as a convenient, neutral and acceptable reference' to the MST.[124]

A more convincing approach has been adopted by a number of other writers who suggest that the growing use of the term FET by Western States in their BITs was intended to counter the assertion made by developing States about the inexistence of any MST under international law.[125] Thus, Western States started including references to the FET standard *because* of the ambiguities surrounding the concept of the MST.[126] They started using this term as a result of the challenge mounted by developing States against the MST.

Weiler provides a detailed account explaining that the US started using the expression FET after the War in its investment treaty negotiation because it had already been used in its commercial and reciprocal trade treaties and

121 Kill (n 11) 879.

122 Newcombe & Paradell (n 11) 263–264.

123 *AWG Group v. Argentina*, UNCITRAL, Decision on Liability, 30 July 2010, Judge Nikken's separate opinion [14–15]: 'Therefore, it is not so easy to say that the concept of international minimum standard was a *well-established* concept. It certainly was for the capital-exporting countries, but not for the rest of the world (...) Clauses on the treatment of foreign investment referring to the "international minimum standard" could hardly be agreed upon, as some of the Parties to those treaties were not willing to accept it *expressis verbi*. "International minimum standard" was a "forbidden phrase" in a treaty for the very many countries that had rejected that standard, because it was associated with unjust international relations, as has been recognized by scholars who have addressed the issue. The explanation suggested by the NAFTA Free Trade Commission interpretation, which reveals the intention of the NAFTA Parties to consider fair and equitable treatment and international minimum standard as identical, was that a formula had to be found for saying the same thing but with different words, neutral words, which were not historically demonized. The phrase "fair and equitable treatment" is a neutral expression in relation to which there was no controversy and it had been used in another context in the Havana Charter signed in 1948 and in the Economic Agreement of Bogota, also signed in 1948'.

124 Newcombe & Paradell (n 11) 263–264. See also: Montt (n 113) 69–70.

125 See, the analysis of Thomas (n 11) 48. *Contra*: Paparinskis (n 1) 163.

126 Weiler (n 1) 199, 211–212, 216, 227, 239–240; Vasciannie (n 88) 157–158.

it was a familiar diplomatic term of art.[127] Recent research have indeed shown that the term 'just and equitable treatment' was used by the US in diplomatic correspondence with other States in the 1930s regarding protection of its nationals abroad.[128] Having examined these commercial treaties in some detail, Weiler concludes that their common thread had been the 'objective of promoting equality of access and non-discrimination for Americans in the decision-making of foreign States and State enterprises'.[129] For him, 'it should be unsurprising, therefore, that the FET clause was pressed into service when officials were casting about for treaty terms that could be used to broaden and deepen access and protection for U.S. investors abroad.'[130] There was also another reason for using the expression:

> Given how the global political atmosphere of the 1950's and 1960's was not conducive to safeguarding private foreign investment, U.S. Department of State officials did not hesitate in offering the more ambiguous FET language in their model treaties, rather than resigning themselves to a perpetual debate over the scope and meaning of the [MST].[131]

The term 'equitable' was indeed attractive to US treaty drafters after the Second World War because 'it [was] capable of bearing multiple meanings'[132] and could 'mean different things to different people'.[133] Thus, while it could be construed as a manifestation of the principle of sovereign equality of States for some, others could rely on it to further legal protection to foreign investors.[134] Yet, as explained by Weiler, in the context of BIT negotiation Western States 'shared the same agenda: use all available legal means to boost the standard of treatment owed to foreign investors'.[135] For him, 'it should also appear beyond doubt that they were not confusing the FET standard with the [MST] in their own minds, although they were undoubtedly hopeful that their official from less developed countries might not be savvy to these interpretative slights of hand'.[136] For Western States, 'it was essential to identify treaty terms capable

127 Weiler, ibid., 191, 194.
128 Blandford (n 59) 300ff.
129 Weiler (n 1) 195.
130 Ibid., 199.
131 Ibid., 199.
132 Ibid., 205.
133 Ibid., 199.
134 Ibid., 199.
135 Ibid., 211.
136 Ibid., 211–2.

of acceptance by potential treaty partners whilst nonetheless ginning up the discretion of future arbitrators to apply more stringent norms of establishment and protection.'[137] In other words, U.S. negotiators embraced the FET standard in the 1960s because the MST 'controversy had otherwise poisoned the well for treaty drafters'.[138] The point is well-explained by Vandevelde:

> Full protection and security had been identified as an element of customary international law since the inter-war FCNs, though it was then called 'most constant protection and security.' During the 1950s, with the concept of an international minimum standard under attack, the United States moved away from references to customary law in its FCNs and sought to establish new standards of a requirement of fair and equitable treatment and a prohibition on arbitrary and discriminatory treatment to complement the most constant protection and security standard.[139]

The actual drafting language used by States in their BITs supports this approach. As pointed out by two authors, 'if the parties to a treaty want to refer to customary international law, one would assume that they will refer to it as such rather than using a different expression'.[140] For the vast majority of BITs that contain an FET clause that does *not* make any reference to international law, the standard should *not* be considered as an implicit reference to the MST.[141] As pointed out by two writers, '[a]s a matter of textual interpretation, it seems implausible that a treaty would refer to a well-known concept like the "minimum standard of treatment in customary international law" by using the expression "fair and equitable treatment"'.[142] This is especially the case considering the (above-mentioned) contentious debates between developed and developing States as to the very existence of an MST.[143]

---

137 Ibid., 211.

138 Ibid., 215.

139 K. Vandevelde, *United States International Investment Agreements* (Kluwer 2002), 263.

140 Schreuer & Dolzer (n 35) 124. See also: Bronfman (n 11) 621; Laviec (n 11) 94; Salacuse (n 11) 226; Vasciannie (n 88) 105; UNCTAD (n 17) 13.

141 UNCTAD (n 17) 13.

142 Schreuer & Dolzer (n 35) 124. See also: Bronfman (n 11) 621; Laviec (n 11) 94; Salacuse (n 11) 226; Vasciannie (n 88) 105; UNCTAD (n 17) 13. This position is adopted in: *Suez* (n 6) [184], but rejected in the Separate opinion of Nikken [10ff].

143 Diehl (n 1) 151; Vasciannie (n 88) 131; UNCTAD (n 17) 13; Salacuse (n 11) 226–7.

2.3 FET should be Considered as a Treaty Standard Independent from the MST, except in Specific Situations

As a result of the historical analysis examined in the previous section, the FET standard should *generally* be considered as an *independent* treaty standard having an autonomous meaning from the MST. This is the position adopted by the majority of writers.[144] It should be noted, however, that a number of scholars have rejected this interpretation.[145] In my view, interpreting FET as an independent treaty standard is certainly the better approach when the clause is unqualified and contains no reference whatsoever to international law.[146]

144 F.A. Mann, 'British Treaties for the Promotion and Protection of Investments', (1981) 52 British YIL 241, 244 ('The terms "fair and equitable treatment" envisage conduct which goes far beyond the minimum standard and afford protection to a greater extent and according to a much more objective standard than any previously employed form of words. A tribunal would not be concerned with a minimum, maximum or average standard. It will have to decide whether in all the circumstances the conduct in issue is fair and equitable or unfair and inequitable. No standard defined by other words is likely to be material. The terms are to be understood and applied independently and autonomously'); Newcombe & Paradell (n 11) 263; Dolzer & Stevens (n 11) 60; Vasciannie (n 88) 144 ('These considerations point ultimately towards the conclusion that the two standards in question are not identical: both standards may overlap significantly with respect to issues such as arbitrary treatment, discrimination and unreasonableness, but the presence of a provision assuring fair and equitable treatment in an investment instrument does not automatically incorporate the international minimum standard for foreign investors'); P. Muchlinski, *Multinational Enterprises and the Law* (2nd ed. Oxford UP 2007) 635–647; McLachlan et al (n 82) 226–247; Dolzer & Schreuer (n 35) 124–128; Tudor (n 1) 53–104; Diehl (n 1) 151–152; C. Schreuer, 'Fair and Equitable Standard (FET): Interaction with Other Standards', (2007) 4(5) TDM; R. Dolzer, 'Fair and Equitable Treatment: A Key Standard in Investment Treaties', (2005) 39(1) Int'l Law, 360; Haeri (n 26) 34; Kinnear (n 40) 7; Margaret Clare Ryan, 'Glamis Gold, Ltd. v. The United States and the Fair and Equitable Treatment Standard', (2011) 56(4) McGill LJ 932–934; Salacuse (n 11) 226–227: Roy Preiswerk, 'New Developments in Bilateral Investment Protection – With Special Reference to Belgian Practice', (1967) 3 RBDI 173, 186; Nigel Blackaby, Constantine Partasides, Alan Redfern & J. Martin H. Hunter, *Redfern and Hunter on International Arbitration*, 494 (Oxford UP 2009).

145 Picherack (n 11) 260–262, 265, 291; Thomas (n 11) 50; Mayeda (n 11) 273–291; Orellana (n 11) 7; Barnali Choudhury, 'Evolution or Devolution? Defining Fair and Equitable Treatment in International Investment Law', (2005) 6(2) J. World Invest. & Trade 317–320; Sornarajah (n 12) 170ff; Charles Leben, 'L'évolution du Droit International des Investissements', in: SFDI, *Un accord multilatéral sur l'investissement: d'un forum de négociation à l'autre?* (1999) 7–28; Maximo Romero Jiménez, 'Considerations of NAFTA Chapter II' (2001) 2 Chicago JIL 243, 244; Paparinskis (n 1) 163; Montt (n 113) 302–310.

146 Kläger (n 1) 61; Haeri (n 26) 33 ('Thus, absent specific treaty wording linking the fair and equitable treatment standard with the international minimum standard in customary

Yet, as logical and sound as it may be, this interpretation is *not* convincing *in certain particular cases* where a treaty *explicitly* links the FET to the standard existing under 'international law'. What was the actual intention of the parties when they made reference to those terms? In the present author's view, any possible ambiguities disappear when there is clear and undeniable evidence that the intention of the State parties was in fact that the FET standard be considered as a reference to the MST under custom.[147] This is clearly the case under NAFTA Article 1105.[148]

Under Article 1105, the FET standard must be considered as *one of the elements* included in the umbrella concept of the MST. In fact, this is evident because the provision requires NAFTA Parties to provide foreign investors treatment in accordance with 'international law', *including* FET. NAFTA tribunals have endorsed this approach.[149] Moreover, as further discussed below, the NAFTA parties have expressly stated that their intention was in fact for the FET standard to make reference to the MST under custom.[150]

3 *The 'Return' of the MST*

Section 3 examines the phenomenon of the 'return' of the MST. As mentioned before, by the year 2000, the majority of BITs contained a stand-alone (or autonomous) reference to the FET standard instead of the MST. By then, the concept of the MST had clearly lost its once prevailing importance as a source of

---

international law, the better view is that the fair and equitable treatment standard is an autonomous standard. In such circumstances, the fair and equitable treatment standard cannot be construed as a reference to the international minimum standard in customary international law'); C. Schreuer, 'Fair and Equitable Treatment in Arbitral Practice', (2005) 6 J. World Invest. & Trade, 363–366, 365, 385 ('in the context of the NAFTA, it is now established that the term as used in Article 1105(1) therein is no more than a reference to established principles of international law. In other contexts, notably that of BITs' the answer depends on the wording of the particular clause. In the absence of indications to the contrary, the better view is to give it an autonomous meaning').

147 The technique of reference (*renvoi*) is often used in treaties: Paparinskis (n 1) 160.

148 Dumberry (n 2) 44–46.

149 Dumberry (n 2) 44, referring to many cases, including *United Parcel Service of America Inc.* v. *Canada*, UNCITRAL, Award on Jurisdiction, 22 November 2002 [97] ('the obligation to accord fair and equitable treatment is not in addition to or beyond the minimum standard. Our reasons in brief are, first, that that reading accords with the ordinary meaning of article 1105. That obligation is "included" within the minimum standard'); *Cargill* (n 7) [296] ('In summation, the Tribunal finds that the obligations in Article 1105(1) of the NAFTA are to be understood by reference to the customary international law minimum standard of treatment of aliens. The requirement of fair and equitable treatment is one aspect of this minimum standard.').

150 See, FTC Note of Interpretation of 2001 (n 9).

investment protection for foreign investors. One could have assumed at the time that the MST's role would become limited to the traditional function played by customary rules under international law in the context of the proliferation of treaty norms. The MST would, for instance, remain the applicable legal regime of protection in the absence of any BIT and could also play a gap-filling role whenever a treaty, a contract or domestic legislation was silent on a given issue.[151] In any event, it was clear that the MST's role in the realm of investment treaty protection was becoming more negligible than ever before in its long history. The MST's glory days were long gone.

Yet, instead of slowly disappearing and becoming somewhat irrelevant, the MST unexpectedly made a comeback as a result of the broad interpretation which was given by arbitral tribunals to FET clauses (Section 3.1.). The following section will examine how States have reacted to these controversial awards and the fact that they began to refer explicitly to the MST in FET clauses contained in their investment treaties with the clear aim to limit the scope of investors' rights under said clauses (Section 3.2.). Finally, I will analyze the FET clause contained in the CETA, which includes a detailed list of the elements considered to be in breach of the standard (Section 3.3.).

3.1 The Broad Interpretation Given to FET Clauses by Arbitral Tribunals and the Importance They Gave to the Terms Used under These Provisions

When arbitral tribunals started to interpret FET clauses that had systematically been included in BITs for decades, States were considerably surprised by the outcome. The controversy began in the year 2000 when three tribunals rendered awards that defined different aspects of the scope of the FET clause (Article 1105) contained in the NAFTA.[152] The *Metalclad* Tribunal found that Mexico had failed to ensure a transparent and predictable framework for the investor's investment, which constituted a breach of Article 1105.[153] Soon after, the majority of the *S.D. Myers* Tribunal came to the conclusion that a finding of a breach of the national treatment provision (Article 1102) established a breach of Article 1105 as well.[154] Finally, and most importantly, the *Pope &*

151 International Law Commission, 'First Report on Formation and Evidence of Customary International Law', by Michael Wood, Special Rapporteur, ILC Sixty-fifth session, Geneva (6 May–7 June and 8 July–9 August 2013) UN Doc. A/CN.4/663. More generally on the question of customary rules in international investment law, see: Dumberry (n 3).

152 On this debate, see, Dumberry (n 2) 65ff.

153 *Metalclad Corporation v. Mexico*, ICSID Case No. ARB(AF)/97/1, Award, 30 August 2000 [70, 76].

154 *S.D. Myers* (n 38) [266].

Talbot Tribunal held, *inter alia*, that Article 1105 requires the application of the FET standard *independently* (and in *addition*) to the MST under international law.[155]

In sum, these three NAFTA tribunals interpreted the FET clause as providing investors with treatment protections *above and beyond* the MST. In other words, under this approach, the level of the standard of treatment imposed on the host State would be *more extensive* than that existing under custom; foreign investors would be given *more rights*. Most importantly, these three tribunals adopted this approach notwithstanding the important fact that under Article 1105 (entitled 'MST') the FET is clearly linked to the standard existing under 'international law'. In fact, all along NAFTA parties had argued in their pleadings that the FET standard was a direct reference to the MST under custom. Both the United States[156] and Canada[157] did so *well before* the issue became controversial.

This NAFTA debate highlights the importance of the actual wording used in FET clauses. Arbitral tribunals (outside the NAFTA context) have given different interpretations to the scope of FET clauses depending on their actual drafting.[158] This is the conclusion reached by a 2004 OECD paper:

---

155 *Pope & Talbot Inc. v. Canada*, UNCITRAL, Award in Respect of Damages, 31 May 2002.

156 In a statement made by the US State Department to the Senate, the 'no less' FET clause contained in the 1992 US Model BIT (referring to 'international law') was described as setting 'a minimum standard of treatment based on customary international law'. See: Description of the United States Model Bilateral Investment Treaty (BIT) – February 1992, Submitted by the State Department, 30 July 1992, in: Hearing before the Committee on the Foreign Relations, United States Senate, 102nd Congress, Second Session, 4 Aug. 1992, S. HRG. 102–795, at 62 (quoted in: Newcombe & Paradell (n 11) 269). The same position was also taken in five so-called 'Letters of Submittal' sent by the US State Department to the US President in 1993 requesting approval of the BITs by the US Senate. See: US-Kazakhstan BIT (1994), Letter of Submittal, 4 September 1993; US-Armenia BIT (1996), Letter of Submittal, 27 August 1993; US-Kyrgyzstan BIT (1994), Letter of Submittal, 7 September 1993; US-Moldova BIT (1994), Letter of Submittal, 25 August 1993; US-Ecuador BIT (1997), Letter of Submittal, 7 September 1993. After 1994, all 'Letters of Submittal' sent by the U.S. State Department would systematically contain the same phrase stating that the terms 'international law' constitutes a reference to the MST under custom (the letters can be found at this page of the website of the Office of the United States Trade Representative: http://tcc.export.gov/Trade_Agreements/Bilateral_Investment_Treaties/index.asp).

157 Department of External Affairs, NAFTA, 'Canadian Statement on Implementation' Canada Gazette, 1 January 1994, 68, 149, explaining that the FET obligation under Article 1105 constitutes a reference to a 'minimum absolute standard of treatment, based on long-standing principles of customary international law'.

158 Newcombe & Paradell (n 11) 263–264; Paparinskis (n 1) 94.

> Because of the differences in its formulation, the proper interpretation of the 'fair and equitable treatment' standard depends on the specific wording of the particular treaty, its context, the object and purpose of the treaty, as well as on negotiating history or other indications of the parties' intent. For example, some treaties include explicit language linking or, in some cases limiting, fair and equitable treatment to the minimum standard of international customary law. Other treaties which either link the standard to international law without specifying custom, or lack any reference to international law, could, depending on the context of the parties' intent, for example, be read as giving the standard a scope of application that is broader than the minimum standard as defined by international customary law.[159]

A 2012 UNCTAD report indicated that the drafting variations in FET clauses have in fact been interpreted as meaning *different content* as well as *different thresholds*:

> [The] identification of the correct source of the FET standard—whether it is grounded in customary international law or is a self-standing obligation—can have important consequences in terms of the standard's content and, more precisely, of the types of State measures that can be challenged as well as the required threshold for finding a violation, that is, the required degree of seriousness of the breach.[160]

Many arbitral tribunals have thus interpreted an unqualified (or 'stand-alone') FET clause as 'delinked from customary international law' and have therefore 'focused on the plain-meaning of the terms "fair" and "equitable,"' which 'may result in a low liability threshold and brings with it a risk for State regulatory action to be found in breach of it'.[161] This phenomenon has been recognized

159 OECD (n 22) 40. See also: Katia Yannaca-Small, 'Fair and Equitable Treatment Standard: Recent Developments', in A. Reinisch (ed), *Standards of Investment Protection*, (Oxford UP 2008) 113–114.

160 UNCTAD (n 17) 8.

161 Ibid., 22, referring to several cases. Recent examples include: *Ioan Micula, Viorel Micula, S.C. European Food S.A, S C. Starmill S.R.L. and S.C. Multipack S.R.L. v. Romania*, ICSID Case No. ARB/05/20, Final Award, 11 December 2013 [503ff]; *ECE* (n 10) [4.756, 4.760]; *Deutsche Bank* (n 10) [417–8]; *Cervin Investissements S.A. and Rhone Investissements S.A. v. Costa Rica*, ICSID Case No. ARB/13/2, Award, 7 March 2017 [452–3]; *Teinver* (n 10) [666].

by many scholars.[162] The vast majority of tribunals have in fact interpreted an unqualified FET clause as having an autonomous character, which therefore provides a higher level of standard of treatment than the MST.[163] In fact, only a limited number of tribunals have interpreted an unqualified FET standard as an implicit reference to international law.[164]

A good illustration is the Tribunal's reasoning in *Saluka*, which held that the FET standard had an autonomous character in the specific context of the BIT at hand precisely because it was not linked to international law.[165] The tribunal

---

162 Haeri (n 26) 26; R. Dolzer, 'Fair And Equitable Treatment International Law, Remarks' (2006) 100 ASIL Proc. 69; Christopher F. Dugan, Don Wallace, Jr., Noah Rubins & Borzu Sabahi, *Investor-State Arbitration* (Oxford UP 2008) 496; Schreuer & Dolzer (n 35) 126; Kläger (n 1) 85. On the contrary, see the position adopted by the following writers: Stephan Schill, 'Fair and Equitable Treatment as an Embodiment of the Rule of Law', in R. Hofmann & C. Tams (eds), *The International Convention on the Settlement of Investment Disputes (ICSID): Taking Stock after 40 Years* (Nomos 2007) (stating that it is 'questionable whether substantial differences result from the different framing of the standard with a view to the actual practice of investment tribunals'); Kenneth J. Vandevelde, 'A Unified Theory of Fair and Equitable Treatment' (2010) 43 NYU J. Int'l L. & Pol. 47 ('Differences in the contexts in which the standard appears have made little difference to tribunals interpreting the standard. Rather, the awards have yielded a single coherent theory of the standard, although perhaps not consciously so').

163 See Newcombe & Paradell (n 11) 263–264, referring to the following cases: *MTD Equity Sdn. Bhd. & MTD Chile S.A. v. Chile*, ICSID Case No. ARB/01/7, Award, 25 May 2004 [110–112]; *Occidental* (n 10) [188–190]; *CMS* (n 6) [282–284]; *Saluka* (n 6) [286–295]; *LG&E* (n 6) [125–131]; *PSEG Global Inc. and Konya Ilgin Elektrik Üretim ve Ticaret Limited Şirketi v. Turkey*, ICSID Case No. ARB/02/5, Award, 19 January 2007 [239]. See also: *Liman Caspian Oil BV and NCL Dutch Investment BV v. Kazakhstan*, ICSID Case No. ARB/07/14, Award, 22 June 2010 [263]; *Inmaris Perestroika Sailing Maritime Services GmbH and others v. Ukraine*, ICSID Case No. ARB/08/8, Award, 1 March 2012 [264–5]. Recent cases include *Philip Morris* (n 52) [316] (indicating that such a clause 'does not mean that the BIT creates an "autonomous" FET standard', but also adding that 'In the absence of any additional qualifying language, the reference to FET in Article 3(2) cannot be read as "treatment required by the minimum standard of treatment under international law").

164 *See*, for instance, *Siemens* (n 10) [291]. Other awards contain more ambiguous language: *BG Group plc v. Argentina*, UNCITRAL, Final Award, 24 December 2007 [290–1]; *Bernhard von Pezold and Others v. Zimbabwe*, ICSID Case No. ARB/10/15, Award, 28 July 2015 [546] ('To the extent FET incorporates the minimum standard of treatment under international law, it is clear that this standard has moved on since the Neer case' (see also at [522] referring to the position of the Claimant).

165 *Saluka* (n 6) [294]: '[Article 3.1 of the Treaty] omits any express reference to the customary minimum standard. The interpretation of Article 3.1 does not therefore share the difficulties that may arise under treaties (such as the NAFTA) which expressly tie the "fair and

added that in the context of such an autonomous FET clause, 'in order to violate the standard, it may be sufficient that States' conduct displays a relatively lower degree of inappropriateness'[166] while in contrast, under the minimum standard, 'in order to violate that standard, States' conduct may have to display a relatively higher degree of inappropriateness'.[167]

This situation contrasts with the rather confusing approach adopted by tribunals faced with an FET clause containing an explicit reference to 'international law'. Tribunals have overall been divided on the proper interpretation and use of these words. While some tribunals have held that the term 'international law' found in an FET clause was a reference to the minimum standard under custom,[168] others have interpreted such an express reference in much the same way as an unqualified FET standard.[169] Others have simply decided not to take position on the issue.[170] The situation has been well-explained by the *El Paso* Tribunal:

> As far as the relation between FET and the minimum standard of international law is concerned, two main approaches have been adopted by ICSID tribunals, to which one may add an intermediate, undecided position.
>
> Under the first approach, FET has to be equated with the minimum standard of treatment provided for by general international law. This has been, for example, the position adopted by the CMS tribunal (…)
>
> The second approach deals with FET as an autonomous concept, considered in general as more demanding and more protective of investors' rights than the minimum standard of treatment provided for by general international law. The Azurix tribunal, for example, took this position (…)

---

equitable treatment" standard to the customary minimum standard. Avoidance of these difficulties may even be regarded as the very purpose of the lack of a reference to an international standard in the Treaty. This clearly points to the autonomous character of a "fair and equitable treatment" standard such as the one laid down in Article 3.1 of the Treaty'.

166 Ibid., [293].

167 Ibid., [292].

168 See, in particular, *M.C.I. Power Group L.C. and New Turbine, Inc. v. Ecuador*, ICSID No. ARB/03/6, Award, 31 July 2007 [369]; *Gold Reserve* (n 52) [567] (see also [555]).

169 *See*, for instance, *Compañía de Aguas* (n 6) [7.4.5ff]; *Técnicas Medioambientales Tecmed, S.A. v. Mexico*, ICSID No. ARB(AF)/00/2, Award, 29 May 2003 [155]; *Crystallex* (n 10) [530]; *Arif* (n 10) [529]; *Total* (n 10) [125]; *Oko Pankki* (n 10) [216, 231–7].

170 One recent example is: *Peter A. Allard v. Barbados*, PCA Case No. 2012-06, Award, 27 June 2017 [193].

Between these two approaches, some tribunals chose not to decide. This was the case of the tribunal in BG v. Argentina which adopted the following position (…)

The Tribunal considers this discussion to be somewhat futile, as the scope and content of the minimum standard of international law is as little defined as the BITS' FET standard, and as the true question is to decide what substantive protection is granted to foreign investors through the FET. The issue is not one of comparing two undefined or weakly defined standards; it is to ascertain the content and define the BIT standard of fair and equitable treatment.

This being said, it is the view of the Tribunal that the position according to which FET is equivalent to the international minimum standard is more in line with the evolution of investment law and international law and with the identical role assigned to FET and to the international minimum standard. The Tribunal wishes to emphasise what is, in its view, the specific role played by both the general international minimum standard and the FET standard as found in BITS. The role of these similar standards is to ensure that the treatment of foreign investments, which are protected by the national treatment and the most-favoured investors' clauses, do not fall below a certain minimum, in case the two mentioned standards do not live up to that minimum. (…)

In conclusion, it is the Tribunal's view that the FET is not to be viewed with reference to national law – in which case it could be lower than required by international law – but has to be interpreted with reference to international law, the result being that it cannot go below what is required by international law, which is the standard to be applied. But if national law or the treatment accorded to some foreigners exceeds this minimum international standard, it is one of the former that has to be applied. In a sense, it could be said that the foreign investor is entitled to the most favourable treatment, be it national law, rules applied to some foreigners or the international minimum standard embodied in FET. The Tribunal thus considers that the FET of the BIT is the international minimum standard required by international law, regardless of the protection afforded by the national legal orders.[171]

The same assessment can be made with regards to FET clauses containing a slightly different reference to international law: 'investment shall at all times be accorded fair and equitable treatment … and shall in no case be accorded

171 *El Paso* (n 6) [331–337].

treatment less than that required by international law'. Under such a so-called 'no less' FET clause, the FET standard is *not* directly linked or attached to the level of treatment existing under international law; international law only sets a floor below which State actions are considered illegal.[172] A number of tribunals have interpreted such a clause in much the same way as an autonomous FET clause, thus requiring a treatment 'additional to, or beyond that of, customary law'.[173] Other tribunals have, on the contrary, held that such a clause provides for a standard of protection no different than that of the MST under custom.[174]

To add to the general confusion, some tribunals have recently concluded that this long-standing debate had only minimal practical relevance.[175] Thus, for tribunals adopting the 'convergence theory', the level of treatment to be accorded to foreign investors under the MST has apparently rapidly evolved in recent years and is therefore said to now be the same as the one existing under BITs containing an unqualified FET clause.[176] I have explained elsewhere,[177] that there are good reasons to believe that the MST under custom has *not* converged with the free-standing FET standard contained in many BITs.[178]

The importance of the distinction between differently-worded FET clauses is also clear from the present author's own analysis of awards interpreting NAFTA Article 1105 (whereby the FET standard is linked to international law).[179] Thus, NAFTA tribunals have consistently held (with a few exceptions) that only

172 I. Laird, 'Betrayal, Shock and Outrage – Recent Developments in NAFTA Article 1105', in T. Weiler (ed.), *NAFTA Investment Law and Arbitration: Past Issues, Current Practice, Future Prospects* (Transnational Publ., 2004) 51; Picherack (n 11) 260; L. Paradell, 'The BIT Experience of The Fair And Equitable Treatment Standard', in Federico Ortino et al. (eds), *Investment Treaty Law, Current Issues II* (British IICL 2007) 123; Vandevelde (n 162) 47.

173 *Enron* (n 6) [258]; *Sempra* (n 6) [302]; *Azurix* (n 6) [361]; *Lemire* (n 10) [253–254]; *Continental Casualty* (n 6) [254]; *Cargill, Incorporated v. Poland*, ICSID Case No. ARB(AF)/04/2, Award, 5 March 2008 [453]; *Total* (n 10) [125]; *EDF* (n 6) [999ff].

174 *Occidental* (n 10) [188–190]; *Lauder* (n 10) [292]; *Alex Genin, Eastern Credit Limited, Inc. and A.S. Baltoil Genin v. Estonia*, Award, 25 June 2001 [367]; *Ulysseas* (n 6) [245]; OI *European* (n 54) [483, 491].

175 *Saluka* (n 6) [291]. See also: UNCTAD (n 17) at 90. See also the reasoning in: *SAUR* (n 6) [490–4]; *Deutsche* (n 10) [419].

176 See, *inter alia*, CMS (n 6) 282–284; *Occidental* (n 10) [190]; *Biwater Gauff* (n 6) [592]; *Duke* (n 6) [333]; *Rumeli* (n 6) [611]; *Rusoro* (n 10) [520–1]; *Murphy* (n 10) [206–208]. This is also the case of *Merrill & Ring* (n 7) [189ff]. For a critical analysis of this case on this specific aspect, see: Dumberry (n 2) 113ff.

177 Dumberry (n 2) 113ff.

178 For a critical analysis of these awards, see: Kill (n 11) 853; UNCTAD (n 87) 75.

179 Dumberry (n 2) 260ff.

the prohibition of arbitrary conduct, denial of justice and the obligation of due process are unambiguously 'elements' of legal protection under this provision. The content of Article 1105 is thus significantly different than that of stand-alone FET clauses found in most BITs. Tribunals interpreting these clauses have been increasingly willing to recognize new requirements as components of the ever-enlarged concept of FET.[180] Prime examples are the 'obligation' to provide a stable and predictable business environment and transparency[181] as well as to protect an investor's legitimate expectations.[182] NAFTA tribunals have adopted a narrower interpretation of the FET precisely because the standard under Article 1105 refers to the level of protection existing under the MST. Thus, the concepts of transparency and legitimate expectations are considered by the vast majority of NAFTA tribunals only as 'factors' to be taken into account when assessing whether or not other well-established elements of the FET standard have been breached.[183] The vast majority of NAFTA tribunals have also emphasized that a high threshold of severity and gravity is required in order to conclude that the host State has breached any of the elements contained within the FET standard under Article 1105.[184] In sum, my analysis of NAFTA Article 1105 confirms that drafting differences do matter in terms of the actual level of protection existing under an FET clause.

---

180 Picherack (n 11) 271.

181 Recent (non-NAFTA) awards recognising such an obligation as part of the FET standard include: *Murphy* (n 10) [206–207]; *Eiser Infrastructure Limited and Energía Solar Luxembourg S.à r.l. v. Spain*, ICSID Case No. ARB/13/36, Final Award, 4 May 2017 [382]; *Blusun S.A., Jean-Pierre Lecorcier and Michael Stein v. Italia*, ICSID Case No. ARB/14/3, Final Award, 27 December 2016 [315(c)]; *Philip Morris* (n 52) [422].

182 See, the analysis in: Florian Dupuy & Pierre-Marie Dupuy, 'What to Expect from Legitimate Expectations? A Critical Appraisal and Look into the Future of the 'Legitimate Expectations' Doctrine in International Investment Law', in Mohamed Abdel Raouf, Philippe Leboulanger, & Nassib G. Ziadé (eds), *Festschrift Ahmed Sadek El-Kosheri: From the Arab World to the Globalization of International Law* (Kluwer 2015), 273–298.

183 Dumberry (n 2) 138–170; P. Dumberry, 'The Protection of Investors' Legitimate Expectations and the Fair and Equitable Treatment Standard under NAFTA Article 1105' (2014) 31(1) J. Int. Arb. 47–74. Another important feature of NAFTA case law is the fact that tribunals have repeatedly narrowly qualified the concept of legitimate expectations in order to significantly reduce its scope of application. It should be added, however, that recently the *Bilcon* Tribunal (n 7) [444–9, 448–9, 455ff, 588–9] came to a different conclusion (see, however, the strong dissenting opinion of Don McRae).

184 Dumberry (n 2) 271. The recent *Bilcon* award (n 7) [440–444], however, applied a much lower threshold to the facts of the case. The same lower threshold also seems to have been adopted by the *Windsteam* Tribunal (n 7) [358, 376, 379].

The next section examines how States were quick to react to various tribunals' broad, and sometimes contradictory, interpretations of FET clauses and the fact that they gave so much importance to the actual terms used in these provisions.

3.2 States' Reactions to These Awards

The above-mentioned broad interpretations of FET clauses adopted by some tribunals led many States to take concrete measures to effectively reduce tribunals' margin of appreciation when assessing the conformity of States' conduct with the FET standard.

The most virulent and comprehensive reaction came from NAFTA parties. Under the aegis of the Free Trade Commission ('FTC'), they responded by issuing the 'Notes of Interpretation of Certain Chapter 11 Provisions' (hereinafter referred to as 'the Note') on July 31st 2001. The Note clarified, *inter alia*, that 'Article 1105(1) prescribes the customary international law minimum standard of treatment of aliens as the minimum standard of treatment to be afforded to investments of investors of another Party' and that the concept of the FET standard does 'not require treatment in addition to or beyond that which is required by the customary international law minimum standard of treatment of aliens'. In other words, the Note interpreted the FET standard *restrictively* by expressly limiting the level of protection to be accorded to foreign investors to the level of protection existing under the MST under custom. The goal of the binding Note was to ensure that no tribunal would ever interpret the FET clause broadly. The Note itself rapidly became the center of an important controversy amongst parties to NAFTA arbitration proceedings, arbitrators and scholars.[185] The present author has examined elsewhere the controversial reasoning of a number of NAFTA tribunals that have in effect challenged the letter and the spirit of the Note by interpreting the concept of customary international law broadly and by emphasizing its evolutionary character.[186]

Around the same time, States also started *explicitly* mentioning in their BITs that the FET standard was not only linked to 'international law', but that it was in fact a reference to the MST under customary international law.[187] Again, two

185 The controversy is examined by the present author in: Dumberry (n 2) 65–80.

186 The issue is examined in: ibid., 89–124; Patrick Dumberry, 'Moving the Goal Post! How Some NAFTA Tribunals have Challenged the FTC Note of Interpretation on the Fair and Equitable Treatment Standard under NAFTA Article 1105' (2014) 8(2) World Arb. & Med. Rev.

187 UNCTAD (n 17) 29.

of the NAFTA Parties (United States and Canada) started this trend when they adopted their respective Model BITs in 2004.[188] For instance, Article 5(1) of the US Model BIT provides that '[e]ach Party shall accord to covered investments treatment in accordance with *customary* international law, including fair and equitable treatment and full protection and security'.[189] Article 5(2) further states that:

> For greater certainty, paragraph 1 prescribes the *customary international law minimum standard of treatment of aliens as the minimum standard of treatment to be afforded to covered investments.* The concepts of 'fair and equitable treatment' and 'full protection and security' do not require treatment in addition to or beyond that which is required by that standard, and do not create additional substantive rights ...[190]

Clearly, Canada and the United States decided to adopt such language to refute the expanding interpretation applied by some NAFTA tribunals and to incorporate the clarification made in the NAFTA FTC Note of 2001.[191] The two BITs that the United States entered into after 2004 with Uruguay and Rwanda also contain the same clause referring specifically to the MST under custom.[192] Recent FTAs that the United States entered into also contain the same FET clause.[193]

---

188 Dumberry (n 2).

189 US Model BIT (2004) (emphasis added). See, Gilbert Gagné & Jean-Frédéric Morin, 'The Evolving American Policy on Investment Protection: Evidence from Recent FTAs and the 2004 Model BIT' (2006) 9 J. Int'l Econ. L. 357.

190 US Model BIT (2004 and 2012) (emphasis added).

191 Céline Lévesque, 'Influences on the Canadian Model FIPA and US Model BIT: NAFTA Chapter 11 and Beyond' (2006) 44 Canadian YIL 255; Kenneth Vandevelde, 'A Comparison of the 2004 and 1994 US Model BITs' (2008–2009) 1 Yb Int'l Invest. L. & Pol. 291; C. Lévesque & A. Newcombe, 'Commentary on the Canadian Model Foreign Promotion and Protection Agreement' in C. Brown (ed.), *Commentaries on Selected Model Investment Treaties* (Oxford UP 2013) 78–80.

192 US-Uruguay BIT (2006), Art. 5(1)(2); US-Rwanda BIT (2012), Art. 5(1)(2).

193 See, Andrew P. Tuck, 'The "Fair And Equitable Treatment" Standard Pursuant to the Investment Provisions of the U.S. Free Trade Agreements with Peru, Colombia and Panama' (2010) 16 L. & Bus. Rev. Am. 385. See, FTAs entered into by the United States with Australia (2004), Central America (CAFTA, 2004), Chile (2003), Morocco (2004) and Singapore (2003, see side letter of 6 May 2003), Oman (2009).

The same is true for recent BITs (and FTAs) that Canada entered into[194] as well as a number of Mexico's BITs.[195]

The *Tamini* Tribunal recently interpreted the US–Oman FTA, which contains the same restrictive language as the US Model BIT, and clearly adopted a narrow approach to the definition of the MST:

> A strict "minimum standard of treatment" provision such as Article 10.5, particularly when considered in the light of Annex 10-A in the present case, cannot be interpreted in the expansive fashion in which some autonomous fair and equitable treatment or full protection and security provisions of other treaties have been interpreted. Indeed, the language of Article 10.5.2 makes very clear that Article 10.5 does "not require treatment in addition to or beyond" that required by the minimum standard of the treatment of aliens under customary international law. (…)
>
> Breach of the minimum standard of treatment thus requires more than a minor derogation from the ideal standard of perfectly fair and equitable treatment (…)
>
> The language of Article 10.5.2 makes it very clear that the State Parties intended to impose only the minimum standard of treatment under customary international law. Whether other treaties impose a different standard of requisite treatment is not the concern of the present Tribunal.[196]

While such specific language is clearly the result of the NAFTA experience, the phenomenon is not limited to the North American context. States in Asia[197] and in Latin America have recently adopted the same types of FET clauses referring to the MST.[198] Many States have also adopted this position in

194 See, Canada-Czech Rep. BIT (2009), Art. 3; Canada-Jordan BIT (2009), Art. 5; Canada-Latvia BIT (2009), Art. 5; Canada-Peru BIT (2006), Art. 5; Canada-Romania BIT (2009), Art. 2; Canada-Slovakia BIT (2010), Art. 3.

195 Australia-Mexico BIT (2005), Protocol, clause 1; Czech Rep.-Mexico BIT (2002), Protocol; Iceland-Mexico BIT (2005); India-Mexico BIT (2007), Art. 5; Trinidad and Tobago-Mexico BIT (2006), Art. 5; United Kingdom-Mexico BIT (2006), Art. 3.

196 *Adel A Hamadi Al Tamimi v. Oman*, ICSID Case No. ARB/11/33, Award, 27 October 2015 [382, 384, 386].

197 UNCTAD (n 17) 25, referring to the Agreement Establishing the ASEAN-Australia-New Zealand Free Trade Area (2009), the Japan-Philippines FTA (2006), China-Peru FTA (2009), Malaysia-New Zealand FTA (2009), India-Korea Comprehensive Economic Partnership Agreement (2009). See also: Korea-Singapore FTA (2006), Art. 10.5; Japan-Laos BIT (2008), Art. 5; Japan-Brunei (2007), Art. 59 (see 'Note').

198 Belgium/Luxembourg-Peru BIT (2005), Art. 3; Chile-Australia FTA (2009), Art. 10.5.

their pleadings. For instance, Guatemala recently argued that the FET clause found in the CAFTA (which contains the same language as the US Model BIT) 'requires only the minimum standard of treatment under customary international law and does not create additional substantive rights'.[199] Many other Latin American States (including Argentina,[200] Ecuador,[201] Paraguay,[202] and Costa Rica[203]) as well as several other States in other continents[204] have also taken the same view. Interestingly, India's new 2015 draft Model BIT does not refer at all to the FET standard, but instead provides protection against a number of elements that are generally considered to be part of the MST under custom (without however specifically referring to the concept per se).[205]

Another recent phenomenon is States becoming 'more precise about the content of the FET obligation and more predictable in its implementation and subsequent interpretation'.[206] One example is the US Model BIT that clarifies that the obligation to provide FET under Article 5(1) 'includes the obligation not to deny justice in criminal, civil, or administrative adjudicatory proceedings in accordance with the principle of due process embodied in the principal legal systems of the world'.[207] This addition is also featured in the United States' most recent BITs and FTAs as well as some of Canada's investment

199 *Railroad* (n 6) [159]. The same position was adopted by El Salvador (ibid., [207–209]) and Honduras (ibid., [207, 211]), both filing submissions as non-disputing States parties during the proceedings.

200 See, for instance: *EDF* (n 6) [343]. In fact, Argentina took that position regardless of the actual FET clause at hand, whether it is an 'autonomous' FET clause or one expressly linked to international law: *BG Group* (n 164) [284, 290]; *National Grid* (n 6) [161]; *Metalpar* (n 6) [117]; *Siemens* (n 10) [289–292]; *Compañía de Aguas* (n 6) [5.2.2., 6.6.2.]; *SAUR* (n 6) [472]; *Total* (n 10) [125].

201 *Chevron* (n 6) [227]; *Ulysseas* (n 6); *MCI Power* (n 6) [250]; *Duke* (n 6) [331].

202 *Bureau Veritas* (n 6) [105, 152–153].

203 *Unglaube* (n 6) [242].

204 See, pleading referred to in these cases: *Saluka* (n 6) [289]; *Biwater Gauff* (n 6) [587]; *Kardassopoulos* (n 6) [409, 417]; *Rumeli* (n 6) [611]; *Bayindir* (n 6) [164, 173].

205 Article 3.1 of the draft Model BIT (available at this page: https://mygov.in/sites/default/files/master_image/Model%20Text%20for%20the%20Indian%20Bilateral%20Investment%20Treaty.pdf) provides protection for 'denial of justice under customary international law', 'Un-remedied and egregious violations of due process' and 'Manifestly abusive treatment involving continuous, unjustified and outrageous coercion or harassment'.

206 UNCTAD (n 17) 29, 13, 30.

207 The Model BIT further specifies at Article 5(3) that 'A determination that there has been a breach of another provision of this Treaty, or of a separate international agreement, does not establish that there has been a breach of this Article'.

treaties.[208] This approach has also been adopted by many other States in the context of ASEAN[209] and COMESA[210] and under the CAFTA-DR (Article 10.5). The text adopted in the context of the TPP is quite similar to the one found in the US Model BIT.[211]

As further examined in the next section, Article 8.10 of the CETA seems to be the natural and logical outcome of States' increasing willingness to narrow the scope of the FET standard and to circumscribe its interpretation by tribunals.[212]

3.3 CETA: the Ultimate Detailed FET Clause

The final text of Article 8.10 (entitled 'Treatment of Investors and of Covered Investments'), contained in the CETA,[213] reads as follows:

1. Each Party shall accord in its territory to covered investments of the other Party and to investors with respect to their covered investments fair and equitable treatment and full protection and security in accordance with paragraphs 2 through 6.
2. A Party breaches the obligation of fair and equitable treatment referenced in paragraph 1 if a measure or series of measures constitutes:
   (a) denial of justice in criminal, civil or administrative proceedings;
   (b) fundamental breach of due process, including a fundamental breach of transparency, in judicial and administrative proceedings.
   (c) Manifest arbitrariness;
   (d) Targeted discrimination on manifestly wrongful grounds, such as gender, race or religious belief;

---

208 David A. Gantz, 'The Evolution of FTA Investment Provisions: From NAFTA to the United States – Chile Free Trade Agreement', (2003) 19(4) Am. U. L. Rev., 724–731. See, for instance, Canada-Colombia FTA (2011), Art. 805; Canada-Romania BIT (2011), Art. II(2).

209 ASEAN Comprehensive Investment Agreement (2009), Art. 11.

210 Investment Agreement for COMESA (2007) Art. 14.

211 Article 9.6.2.

212 Güneş Ünüvar, 'The Vague Meaning of Fair and Equitable Treatment Principle in Investment Arbitration and New Generation Clarifications', iCourts Working Paper Series, No. 55(2), 22; G. Ünüvar, 'Is CETA the Promised Breakthrough? Interpretation and Evolution of Fair and Equitable Treatment and Indirect Expropriation Provisions', in: M Andenas & L Pantaleo (eds), *The EU as an Actor in International Economic Law* (TMC Asser Press 2017).

213 The final text of the agreement was released, following legal review, on February 29, 2016: http://www.international.gc.ca/trade-commerce/trade-agreements-accords-commerciaux/agr-acc/ceta-aecg/index.aspx?lang=eng.

(e) Abusive treatment of investors, such as coercion, duress and harassment; or
(f) A breach of any further elements of the fair and equitable treatment obligation adopted by the Parties in accordance with paragraph 3 of this Article.

3. The Parties shall regularly, or upon request of a Party, review the content of the obligation to provide fair and equitable treatment. The Committee on Services and Investment, established under Article 26.2.1(b) (Specialized Committee), may develop recommendations in this regard and submit them to the CETA Joint Committee for decision.
4. When applying the above fair and equitable treatment obligation, a tribunal may take into account whether a Party made a specific representation to an investor to induce a covered investment, that created a legitimate expectation, and upon which the investor relied in deciding to make or maintain the covered investment, but that the Party subsequently frustrated.
5. For greater certainty, 'full protection and security' refers to the Party's obligations relating to physical security of investors and covered investments.
6. For greater certainty, a breach of another provision of this Agreement, or of a separate international agreement does not establish a breach of this Article.
7. For greater certainty, the fact that a measure breaches domestic law does not, in and of itself, establish a breach of this Article. In order to ascertain whether the measure breaches this Article, the Tribunal must consider whether a Party has acted inconsistently with the obligations in paragraph 1.[214]

When drafting Article 8.10, the parties had in mind the 'alternative way to qualify, clarify and/or narrow down the FET standard' which had been put forward in a 2012 UNCTAD report to 'replace the general FET provision'.[215] Yet, what is

---

214 See: P. Dumberry, 'Fair and Equitable Treatment', in: Stefanie Schacherer & Makane Moïse Mbengue (eds), *Foreign Investment under the Comprehensive Economic and Trade Agreement (CETA)* (Springer 2018).

215 UNCTAD (n 17) 108, listing the following specific obligations: '(a) Denial of justice and flagrant violations of due process; (b) Manifestly arbitrary treatment; (c) Evident discrimination; (d) Manifestly abusive treatment involving continuous, unjustified coercion or harassment; (e) Infringement of legitimate expectations based on investment-inducing representations or measures, on which the investor has relied.'

probably the most striking feature of Article 8.10 is the undeniable fact that the final list of elements it contains (and their actual contours) is to a very large extent based on how NAFTA tribunals have interpreted Article 1105 over the last 20 years.[216]

Article 8.10 is the first FET clause contained in an IIA that specifically enumerates the different situations resulting in a breach of the obligation. This is a *closed list*[217] defining specifically what the parties consider to be the standard. Canada had never before adopted such a FET clause. This is also a first in the European context since the CETA is the first trade agreement containing a comprehensive investment chapter concluded by the EU. This special type of FET clause has now found its way in trade agreements signed by the EU in recent years.[218] Thus, a similar clause is found in the EU-Singapore FTA[219] and in the EU-Vietnam FTA.[220] It should be added that the proposed text of the (now doomed) Transatlantic Trade and Investment Partnership (TTIP) between the EU and the United States also contained an FET clause with similar language to that provided by Article 8.10.[221]

One of the most notable features of Article 8.10 is the important fact that it does *not* refer to the terms MST or to custom.[222] This is quite a novel approach

216 See, Dumberry (n 214). My analysis of NAFTA case law, Dumberry (n 2) 125–275, suggests that only the prohibition of manifest arbitrary conduct, denial of justice and the obligation of due process are unambiguously stand-alone elements of the FET obligation under Article 1105.

217 Whether or not this is actually the case is debatable since the word 'only' does not appear before the enumeration of obligations (See, G. Van Harten, 'The EU-Canada Joint Interpretive Declaration/Instrument on the CETA', Osgoode Legal Studies Research Paper No. 6/2017). In any event, what is clear is that the parties initially intended the list to be non-exhaustive. Thus, the February 2013 draft refers to the EU proposal using the words 'notably' and 'not exclusively' before the list of obligations. Canada's proposal mentioned that it 'includes' such obligations. Such language was not kept in the final text.

218 All documents can be found here: http://ec.europa.eu/trade/policy/countries-and-regions/agreements/.

219 EU-Singapore Free Trade Agreement, signed in 2014, but not yet into force. The May 2015 text can be found here: http://trade.ec.europa.eu/doclib/press/index.cfm?id=961.

220 EU-Vietnam Free Trade Agreement, not yet into force. The Agreed text of January 2016 can be found here: http://trade.ec.europa.eu/doclib/docs/2016/february/tradoc_154210.pdf, http://trade.ec.europa.eu/doclib/press/index.cfm?id=1437.

221 Commission Draft Text TTIP – Investment [TTIP], online: http://trade.ec.europa.eu/doclib/docs/2015/september/tradoc_153807.pdf, see Art. 3.

222 Interestingly, in a previous draft, the parties had included another paragraph indicating that the FET protection could also cover treatment other than those specifically enumerated in the second paragraph if they were 'contrary to the fair and equitable treatment

for Canada since all of its recent investment treaties contain such a reference. The parties certainly believed that there was no need to expressly link the FET to the standard existing under the MST precisely because the clause contains a comprehensive enumeration of the elements they considered to be comprised in the FET 'box'. In my view, such an omission of the terms MST should not be interpreted as a possible setback to the phenomenon of the 'return' of the MST. This is because the list of obligations contained at Article 8.10 is in fact the same as those generally considered to be comprised within the umbrella concept of the MST.[223] One writer has recently referred to Article 8.10 as a MST clause with another name.[224]

4 *Conclusion*

One writer has recently noted that 'tying the FET to customary international law has done little to reduce the uncertainty' about the content and the scope of the standard.[225] There is indeed some truth to that in the NAFTA context.[226] Thus, faced with the binding FTC Note (linking the FET to the MST), several tribunals (*Pope & Talbot, Mondev, ADF* and others) have simply 'moved the goal post'.[227] They have thus interpreted customary international law broadly by emphasizing its evolutionary character. In doing so, these awards have (at least implicitly) challenged the FTC Note. The *Merrill & Ring* Tribunal later took this 'evolutionary' approach to the extreme by adopting the theory of 'convergence'. It held that the MST has evolved so rapidly in recent years to the point where it now (apparently) protects foreign investors 'against all such acts or behaviour

obligation recognized in the general practice of States accepted as law.' This was a clear reference to the concept of custom under international law. This addition essentially acknowledged the evolving nature of the FET standard and the fact that new situations could eventually become contrary to custom in the future. This feature was, however, not kept in the final text. This is most likely because the parties felt that any such evolution could be taken into account by the periodic review mechanism (provided for at [2(f) and 3]) whereby they may add new situations that they consider to be in breach of the standard. On this point, see: U. Kriebaum, 'FET and Expropriation in the Comprehensive Economic Trade Agreement between the European Union and Canada (CETA)', (2016) TDM 21–22.

223 Dumberry (n 3) 104ff.

224 Enrique Boone Barrera, 'The Case for Removing the Fair and Equitable Treatment Standard from NAFTA', (2017) CIGI Papers No. 128, 10.

225 Barrera, ibid., 9.

226 Flavien Jadeau & Fabien Gélinas, 'CETA's Definition of the Fair and Equitable Treatment Standard: Toward a Guided and Constrained Interpretation', (2016) 13(1) TDM 10.

227 Dumberry (n 2) 89–124; Dumberry (n 186).

that might infringe on a sense of fairness, equity and reasonableness'.[228] The adoption of this approach by the *Merrill & Ring* Tribunal is a direct challenge to the FTC Note.[229]

Other tribunals (*Glamis, Cargill*) have taken a different approach. The *Glamis* Tribunal first noted that the 'fundamentals' of the *Neer* standard still apply today and therefore, in order to prove a violation of the MST, an investor must show that the conduct was 'egregious' and 'shocking'.[230] Yet, the Tribunal was quick to add that it was 'entirely possible, however that, as an international community, we may be shocked by State actions now that did not offend us previously'.[231] In other words, while the '*test*' may not have changed, it nevertheless remains that the *perception* regarding what is 'egregious' and 'shocking' has evolved overtime. The type of State conduct that would have not been considered as a breach of the MST in the past may be deemed so today. Whether this is the case is for each tribunal to determine. Nothing prevents a tribunal from adopting a very liberal interpretation of what it considers to be 'egregious' and 'shocking' State conduct.[232] For that reason, I have argued elsewhere that the practical differences between the reasoning adopted by the *Glamis* Tribunal and that of the *Mondev* and *ADF* tribunals may be more apparent than real.[233]

Yet, at the time of writing my book, I noted that these developments had not had any real impact on the actual outcome of the cases in question in terms of liability.[234] For instance, the extremely broad interpretation adopted by the *Merrill* tribunal had not let it to conclude that Canada breached Article 1105. The situation seems rather different today following the *Bilcon* award, where the majority of the Tribunal found Canada to be in violation of this provision *precisely* because it adopted a broad (and highly questionable) interpretation of the evolution of the MST.[235] What the majority of the Tribunal seems to have considered as 'egregious' and 'shocking' conduct may have come as a surprise (and indeed been 'shocking' …) to many observers.

---

228 *Merrill & Ring* (n 7) 210.

229 Dumberry (n 2) 117–122.

230 Glamis (n 7) [616].

231 Ibid. [616].

232 See, C. Lévesque, 'Chronique de Droit international économique en 2010–2011 – Investissement', (2010) 43 Can YIL 311–313.

233 Dumberry (n 2), 106ff.

234 Ibid., 123.

235 Barrera (n 224) 6–7.

For that reason, the degree of specificity of the CETA FET clause is a welcome development. The reference to the MST in BITs (and the FTC Note) has not been entirely successful at harmonizing the interpretation of the standard and limiting its scope.[236] Under the CETA FET clause, a tribunal would no longer have the freedom to simply 'move the goal post' by broadly interpreting how the MST has evolved in recent years. In CETA, the 'evolution' has effectively been *stopped* with the specific enumeration of elements contained in the FET clause.[237] In my view, the clause contains the most appropriate language to limit the discretion of tribunals to define FET widely.

In theory, one could argue that it is still possible for a tribunal (following the *Glamis* example) to give a wide interpretation to any of the specific elements contained in the enumeration set out at Article 8.10. As such, even a closed list of what constitutes an FET breach would not prevent a tribunal like *Merrill & Ring* to interpret the concept of arbitrariness or due process in a very broad manner.[238] Indeed, nothing can prevent a *Bilcon* like-minded tribunal to come up with its own particular view of what it considers to be a 'manifest' or a 'fundamental' breach of the FET standard.[239] Yet, in my view, the possibility of such an outcome is rather unlikely since the CETA has established a permanent Tribunal of first instance and the Appellate Tribunal.[240] This will ensure that the same adjudicators decide on every case, thereby allowing for a more consistent and coherent jurisprudence with regards to the FET standard.[241] This is

236 Jadeau (n 226), 11–12; Ünüvar (n 212) 22–23.

237 There remains, of course, the possibility under Article 8.10.3 for the parties to review and update the content of the standard.

238 See, the comments in: C. Henckels, 'Protecting Regulatory Autonomy Through Greater Precision in Investment Treaties: The TPP, CETA and TTIP', (2017) 19(1) JIEL.

239 E. De Brabandere, 'States' Reassertion of Control Over International Investment Law – (Re)Defining 'Fair and Equitable Treatment' and 'Indirect Expropriation'', in Andreas Kulick (ed.), *States' Reassertion of Control over International Investment Agreements and International Investment Treaty Dispute Settlement* (Cambridge UP 2016), 298 (also in: Grotius Centre Working Paper 2016/55-IEL; Leiden Law School Research Paper).

240 Articles 8.27, 8.28. See, Stefanie Schacherer, 'TPP, CETA and TTIP Between Innovation and Consolidation – Resolving Investor–State Disputes under Mega-Regionals', (2016) 7 J. Int. Disp. Settl. 631; G. Van Harten, 'ISDS in the Revised CETA: Positive Steps, But Is It a "Gold Standard"?', (2016) CIGI Investor-State Arbitration Commentary Series No. 6; A. VanDuzer, 'Investor-State Dispute Settlement in CETA: Is It the Gold Standard?' (2016) C.D. Howe Institute Commentary No. 459; Ottawa Faculty of Law Working Paper No. 2016–44.

241 See, Schacherer, ibid. 642.

the best safeguard against any future attempts by arbitral tribunals to adopt a broad interpretation of the FET standard.[242]

II Has the FET Standard Become a Rule of Customary International Law?

Introduction

As mentioned in the last chapter, one of the most controversial questions debated by scholars (and tribunals) is related to the interaction between the MST and the FET standard. I have argued that the FET standard should *generally* be considered as an *independent* treaty standard with an autonomous meaning from the MST. While this is the preferred approach for most FET clauses, I have also explained that this is not the case for those FET clauses where the standard is *explicitly* linked to 'international law' (or, more rarely, to the MST).

This chapter addresses another related (but distinct) issue: whether or not the FET standard should now be considered *in and of itself* as a rule of customary international law.[243] The basic argument advanced by the supporters of this proposition is the fact that the standard is found in the overwhelming majority of BITS.[244] For Tudor, 'the FET standard became a customary norm of its time: quick in its formation and based essentially on a State practice derived from the treaties signed by an overwhelming number of States, which in the majority contain a FET clause.'[245] As mentioned above, I have conducted my

---

242 Moreover, CETA Article 8.31(3) provides the possibility for the CETA Joint Committee to adopt a binding interpretation 'where serious concerns arise as regards matters of interpretation that may affect investment'.

243 This chapter is a modified and up-to-date version of an article published by the author: Dumberry (n 108) 155–178. See also: Dumberry (n 3) 140ff, 182.

244 Tudor (n 1) 65–68; Diehl (n 1) 10–11, 125–153, 175–179; Alfred Siwy, 'Investment Arbitration – Indirect Expropriation and the Legitimate Expectations of the Investor' in Christian Klausegger *et al.* (eds), *Austrian Arbitration Yearbook 2007* (C.H. Beck, Stämpfli and Manz 2007); Courtney C. Kirkman, 'Fair and Equitable Treatment: Methanex v. United States and the Narrowing Scope of NAFTA Article 1105', (2002–2003) 34 Law & Pol'y Int'l Bus., 392; Todd Weiler, 'NAFTA Investment Arbitration and the Growth of International Economic Law', (2002) 2 Bus. L. Int'l, 188; Laird (n 172) 70–74; Jan Schokkaert & Yvon Heckscher, *International Investments Protection: Comparative Law Analysis of Bilateral and Multilateral Interstate Conventions, Doctrinal Texts and Arbitral Jurisprudence Concerning Foreign Investments* (Bruylant 2009) 331.

245 Tudor (n 1) 85.

own research and found that less than 5% of BITs do not include any formal and binding FET obligation for host States of investments.[246]

Yet, it is not at all self-evident from the fact that the FET is found in the overwhelming majority of BITs that it *necessarily* follows that the standard should be considered as a customary rule. In fact, the opposite conclusion can be drawn. The very fact that States are still consistently signing BITs today containing FET clauses can equally be interpreted as evidence that no such standard of protection exist under custom.[247] Thus, if the FET standard truly existed under custom, it may be argued that States would not need to include such protection in their BITs. In fact, the mere quantitative number of FET clauses (however impressive it might be) does not offer much clue as to its customary character. As noted by the ICJ, 'the frequency or even habitual character of the acts is not in itself enough,' States must 'feel that they are conforming to what amounts to a legal obligation.'[248] Thus, rules of customary international law develop over time based on the uniform and consistent practice of a large number of representative States, which have the conviction (or the belief) that such practice is required by law (*opinio juris*).

I will argue that the FET standard has *not* become a customary rule. While the transformation of the content of provisions contained in treaties into a customary rule has long been recognized under international law, it remains that this phenomenon is rare in practice given the strict conditions under which such a transformation can occur. In an article published recently, I have undertaken the first empirical analysis of the customary status of the FET standard based on the two conditions under which a treaty-based norm can transform into a customary rule.[249] These findings are presented in Section 3.

The two conditions further examined below are the following. First, it needs to be shown that a significantly large number of States have entered into numerous BITs that contain the same provision (or very similarly-drafted clauses). In other words, the practice of States who are *parties* to BITs must be uniform, consistent, and representative. I will show that while the practice of States to include FET clauses in their BITs can be considered as general, widespread and representative, it remains that it is *not* uniform and consistent

---

246 It should be added that the present author has limited his analysis to BITs and has not examined whether or not multilateral investment treaties and free trade agreements contain FET clauses. One study of these treaties (Tudor (n 1) 36–51) shows that the vast majority of them include FET clauses.

247 Weiler (n 1) 236.

248 *North Sea Continental Shelf Cases* (n 19) 44 [77].

249 Dumberry (n 108).

enough for the standard to have crystallised into a customary rule. As already mentioned above, there are in fact many different types of FET clauses and these variations matter a great deal in terms of the level of obligations imposed on host States. Second, it needs to be shown that States have also adopted in their own practice *outside* treaties the type of conduct prescribed for in these instruments. The evidence suggests that this second condition is not fulfilled. My investigation of 165 foreign investment laws shows that States very rarely offer FET protection to foreign investors.[250] Finally, this chapter will show that States also lack the necessary *opinio juris* for any rule of customary law to be said to have emerged. There is indeed no indication that States parties to BITS believe that they have an *obligation* under international law to provide FET protection to each other's investors *notwithstanding* the fact that such protection is often contained in BITS.

Before examining in detail these findings, two preliminary questions will be examined. I will first address the basic question of when does the issue of the customary status of the FET standard actually matters (Section 1.). I will then analyze the position adopted by tribunals on this controversial question (Section 2.).

1 *Situations Where the Question of the Customary Status of the FET Standard is Relevant*

A basic point needs to be addressed at the outset. Thus, the question of whether or not the FET standard can be considered as a rule of custom is *not* relevant in a number of specific situations. For instance, the question is of *no* practical importance in the situation where a BIT exists and regulates the relationship between a foreign investor and the host State and when that treaty contains an FET clause. In such a case, the host State *must* provide the FET standard of protection to the investor. This is a *treaty obligation* binding on the host State. Also, a tribunal will have to apply that clause to an eventual dispute between the parties. In other words, for the actors involved (the investor, the State and the arbitrators) what matters is the existence of the FET clause in the treaty, and not whether the standard can also (in addition) be considered as representing a customary norm outside the BIT framework.[251] In other words, the question of the customary nature of the FET standard will *not* be of great relevance for the overwhelming majority of BITS which *do* contain a FET clause.

250 This specific question is examined in: Patrick Dumberry, 'The Practice of States as Evidence of Custom: Fair and Equitable Treatment Standard Clauses in States' Foreign Investment Laws', (2015–16) 2 McGill JDR 66–81.

251 Kläger (n 1) 260–70.

In fact, the question of the customary status of the FET standard is relevant in two distinct situations.

First, the question is of great importance whenever there is no BIT that governs the relationship between a foreign investor and the host country of the investment. However numerous BITs may be, it remains that, according to some estimates,[252] they only cover some 13% of the total bilateral relationship between States worldwide. The majority of foreign investors doing business abroad are therefore not covered by these treaties. These (unfortunate) investors will nevertheless receive some legal protection under a contract or under the domestic legislation of the country where they invest. They will also benefit from existing customary rules in the field of international investment law.[253] Custom applies to all States, including those which have not entered into any BIT. These rules may be invoked by *any foreign investor* before an arbitral tribunal irrespective of whether or not the State of origin has entered into a BIT with the country where the investment is made.[254] In other words, custom is the applicable legal regime in the absence of any BIT. In this context, it matters a great deal to determine whether or not States are bound to provide an FET protection under custom.

Second, the question of the customary nature of the FET standard is also (to some extent) relevant in cases where a BIT *does* govern the relationship between a foreign investor and the host country, but where that treaty does *not* contain any FET clause. Yet, it should be added that in practice the question of the customary status of the FET standard under this scenario rarely matters for two reasons. The first reason is that only a small minority (about 5%) of BITs do not contain an FET clause. The second reason is the potential impact that a Most Favoured Nation (MFN) clause may have on a BIT which does not contain a FET clause.

Thus, even when a BIT does not include a FET clause, it may be that an investor will be able to invoke the MFN clause contained in that treaty to rely on provisions found in *another* treaty entered into by the host State that provide for a 'better' treatment. This is because a BIT containing an FET clause arguably provides (at least in theory) foreign investors with a 'better' treatment

252 Gazzini (n 11) 691.

253 More generally on the question of customary norms in international investment arbitration, see Dumberry (n 3).

254 One important point to mention is that a customary rule can only be invoked before a tribunal which *has jurisdiction* over a given dispute under a contract or under the domestic legislation of the country where the investment is made. In other words, there is *no custom* rule which can 'create' jurisdiction for a tribunal over a dispute.

than a treaty without such a provision. In other words, in this scenario (i.e. a BIT not containing any FET clause), it is likely that an investor will be able to benefit from an FET protection contained in another treaty via the use of the MFN clause. This is indeed the conclusion reached so far by investment tribunals which have accepted the importation of FET protection through broad MFN clauses.[255] In the present author's view, this should indeed be the case whenever the MFN clause is drafted in very general terms and its scope of application is broad. As a matter of principle, there is no reason to exclude FET protection from the normal application of a broad MFN clause to substantive protections found in treaties.[256] The present author has examined elsewhere all publicly available BITs that do not contain FET clauses (75 treaties) to concretely determine whether or not they include an MFN clause which would allow for such importation.[257] My findings show that all BITs (except for two) contain MFN clauses that are broad enough and under which the importation of FET clauses from other treaties should be allowed.

I have also examined elsewhere the following different (but related) issue: whether a MFN clause contained in the basic treaty which *does* include an FET clause can be used by an investor to claim the benefit of *better* FET protection found in other BITs entered into by the host State.[258] At the heart of the question addressed in that paper is the difficult task of determining precisely what would constitute a 'better' FET clause.[259] I have argued that a stand-alone FET clause provides (at least in theory) 'better' legal protection to a foreign investor than an FET clause linked to 'international law' or the MST under custom. In my view, if an investor can establish the existence of a differently-worded FET clause offering a better level of protection, it should be allowed to use a broad and unrestricted MFN clause to benefit from such protection found in another treaty. Tribunals have so far accepted that proposition. They have held

---

255 The question is examined in detail in P. Dumberry, 'The Importation of the Fair and Equitable Treatment Standard Through MFN Clauses: An Empirical Study of BITs', (2016) 17 ICSID Rev. 229–259, examining the following cases: *Bayindir* (n 6) [148 ff]; *Rumeli* (n 6); *ATA Construction, Industrial and Trading Co v. Jordan*, ICSID Case No. ARB/08/2, Award, 18 May 2010; *L.E.S.I. S.p.A. and ASTALDI S.p.A. v. Algérie*, ICSID Case No. ARB/05/3, Sentence, 12 November 2008. See, however, a more restrictive approach adopted in: *İçkale İnşaat Limited Şirketi v. Turkmenistan*, ICSID Case No. ARB/10/24, Award, 8 March 2016 [326ff].

256 Dumberry, ibid.

257 Ibid.

258 P. Dumberry, 'Shopping for a Better Deal: The Use of MFN Clauses to Get 'Better' Fair and Equitable Treatment Protection', (2016) Arb. Int. 1–16.

259 Paparinskis (n 1) 134; Ziegler (n 21) 101.

that an investor faced with a 'less-advantageous' FET clause (for instance, one where the FET is linked to the MST) could invoke the MFN clause contained in a BIT to obtain the 'better' protection offered by a stand-alone FET clause included in another BIT entered into by the host State.[260] The situation is not different under NAFTA where tribunals have not openly rejected, as a matter of principle, this possibility.[261] These findings are important given the fact that States are increasingly adopting treaties containing FET clauses having a restrictive scope (a point examined below). In any event, the parties to BITs are free to limit the scope of application of an MFN clause in order to precisely prevent such importation.[262] A number of States have begun doing this in recent years.[263]

2 *The Position Adopted by Tribunals on the Customary Status of the Standard*

Only a few tribunals have taken the position that the FET standard has become a rule of customary international law in and of itself. To the best of the present author's knowledge, only NAFTA tribunals have so far discussed the issue in their awards.[264] The first tribunal which openly adopted this view was the NAFTA *Pope and Talbot* Tribunal in its second award of 2002. For the Tribunal, the fact that the FET standard was found in so many BITs basically established the element of State practice necessary to prove the existence of a rule of customary international law:

---

260 See, *MTD Equity* (n 163); *Sergei Paushok, CJSC Golden East Company, CJSC Vostokneftegaz Company v. Mongolia*, UNCITRAL, Award, 28 April 2011.

261 On NAFTA case law, see: P. Dumberry, 'The Importation of 'Better' Fair and Equitable Treatment Standard Protection Through MFN Clauses: An analysis of NAFTA Article 1103' (2017) 14(1) TDM 1–16. The majority of NAFTA tribunals have however held that this importation could not take place given the fact that the level of treatment was the *same* under NAFTA Article 1105 and the FET clauses contained in BITs referred to by the claimants.

262 See, the different drafting options proposed in: UNCTAD, 'Most-Favoured-nation Treatment: A Sequel', UNCTAD Series on Issues in International Investment Agreements II (2010) 12.

263 Thus, Canada's Model BIT (2004) explicitly prevents investors from invoking the MFN clause to get any better treatment under other already existing BITs entered into (or signed) by Canada. Also, under Article 8.7(4) of the CETA, an investor cannot use the MFN clause contained in the agreement to claim the benefit of a better FET clause found in both past and future treaties. It is also noteworthy that India's Draft Model BIT (2015) does not contain a MFN clause.

264 Dumberry (n 2) 119–122.

> Canada's views on the appropriate standard of customary international law for today were perhaps shaped by its erroneous belief that only some 70 bilateral investment treaties have been negotiated, however, the true number, now acknowledged by Canada, is in excess of 1800. Therefore, applying the ordinary rules for determining the content of custom in international law, one must conclude that the practice of states is now represented by those treaties.[265]

The Tribunal's reasoning is controversial and questionable on many grounds. First, the Tribunal completely disregarded the requirement to show States' *opinio juris* to establish the existence of a customary rule. Second, the Tribunal did not discuss at all the actual content of these BITs. These grounds of criticism were echoed in the subsequent NAFTA *ADF* case where the Tribunal made reference to the strong position adopted by the United States[266] and Mexico.[267] In the *Mondev* ruling, the Tribunal also referred to the NAFTA Parties' strong disapproval of the reasoning of the *Pope and Talbot* award on this issue.[268]

The *Mondev* Tribunal mentioned that '[i]t is often difficult in international practice to establish at what point obligations accepted in treaties, multilateral or bilateral, come to condition the content of a rule of customary international law binding on States not party to those treaties.'[269] For the Tribunal, the answer was quite simple: the respondent (United States) had apparently contended that 'when adopting provisions for fair and equitable treatment and full protection and security in NAFTA (as well as in other BITs), the intention

265 *Pope & Talbot* (n 155) [62].

266 *ADF* (n 7) [112]: '[t]he *Pope and Talbot* Tribunal did not examine the mass of existing BITs to determine whether those treaties represent concordant state practice and whether they constitute evidence of the *opinio juris* constituent of customary international law.' For the United States, the *Pope* Tribunal was therefore 'not in a position to state whether any particular BIT obligation has crystallized into a rule of customary international law.'

267 Ibid. [125].

268 *Mondev* (n 7) [110]: 'In their post-hearing submissions, all three NAFTA Parties challenged holdings of the Tribunal in *Pope & Talbot* which find that the content of contemporary international law reflects the concordant provisions of many hundreds of bilateral investment treaties. In particular, attention was drawn to what those three States saw as a failure of the *Pope & Talbot* Tribunal to consider a necessary element of the establishment of a rule of customary international law, namely *opinio juris*. These States appear to question whether the parties to the very large numbers of bilateral investment treaties have acted out of a sense of legal obligation when they include provisions in those treaties such as that for 'fair and equitable' treatment of foreign investment'.

269 Ibid.

was to incorporate principles of customary international law'.[270] The Tribunal concluded, in the NAFTA context, as follows:

> Thus the question is not that of a failure to show *opinio juris* or to amass sufficient evidence demonstrating it. The question rather is: what is the content of customary international law providing for fair and equitable treatment and full protection and security in investment treaties?[271]

This passage is ambiguous. It is not entirely clear whether the Tribunal simply endorsed the position advanced by the United States that the FET standard is a reference to the MST existing under custom or, instead, whether the Tribunal believed that the FET standard had *itself* become a rule of customary international law. There are indeed a few passages in the award that seem to suggest that the Tribunal in fact supported the later position. Thus, the Tribunal mentions that the 2,000 existing BITs 'almost uniformly' contain an FET clause adding that 'such a body of concordant practice will necessarily have influenced the content of rules governing the treatment of foreign investment in current international law.'[272] It also added that the content of 'current international law' was 'shaped by the conclusion of more than two thousand bilateral investment treaties and many treaties of friendship and commerce,' and that 'those treaties largely and concordantly' include an FET clause.[273] This position was later endorsed by the *Chemtura* Tribunal, which stated that the determination of NAFTA Article 1105 'cannot overlook the evolution of customary international law, nor the impact of BITs on this evolution'.[274] In sum, the different statements made by the *Mondev* Tribunal suggest that it endorsed the proposition that this 'uniform' practice of States incorporating FET clauses in their BITs had led to the formation of a rule of custom.[275]

A few months later in 2003, the *ADF* Tribunal stated that while the *Mondev* Tribunal was 'implying that the process was in motion,' it had in fact *not*

270 Ibid.

271 Ibid., [113]. See also [122].

272 Ibid., [117].

273 Ibid., [125].

274 *Chemtura Corporation v. Canada*, UNCITRAL, Award, 2 August 2010 [121].

275 Alexander Orakhelashvili, 'The Normative Basis of "Fair and Equitable Treatment": General International Law on Foreign Investment?' (2008) 1 Archive des Völkerrechts 78; Laird (n 172) 70–7467, 69, 70. See also Stephan W. Schill, 'Fair and Equitable Treatment, the Rule of Law, and Comparative Public Law' in Stephan W. Schill (ed) *International Investment Law and Comparative Public Law* (Oxford UP 2010) 153.

endorsed the position that the FET obligation was a customary rule.[276] In any event, the *ADF* Tribunal expressly rejected the contention (made by the investor in the proceedings) that the FET standard had become part of custom:

> We are not convinced that the Investor has shown the existence, in current customary international law, of a general and autonomous requirement (autonomous, that is, from specific rules addressing particular, limited, contexts) to accord fair and equitable treatment and full protection and security to foreign investments. The Investor, for instance, has not shown that such a requirement has been brought into the corpus of present day customary international law by the many hundreds of bilateral investment treaties now extant. It may be that, in their current state, neither concordant state practice nor judicial or arbitral caselaw provides convincing substantiation (or, for that matter, refutation) of the Investor's position.[277]

The *Merrill & Ring* Tribunal took a different view. It held that 'against the backdrop of the evolution of the minimum standard of treatment' it was 'satisfied that fair and equitable treatment has *become a part of customary law*.'[278] The Tribunal gave the following explanation (without, however, embarking on a concrete analysis of State practice and *opinio juris*[279]):

> A requirement that aliens be treated fairly and equitably in relation to business, trade and investment is the outcome of this changing reality and as such it has become sufficiently part of widespread and consistent practice so as to demonstrate that it is reflected today in customary international law as opinio juris. In the end, the name assigned to the standard does not really matter. What matters is that the standard protects against all such acts or behavior that might infringe a sense of fairness, equity and reasonableness. Of course, the concepts of fairness, equitableness and reasonableness cannot be defined precisely: they require to be applied to the facts of each case. In fact, the concept of fair and equitable treatment has emerged to make possible the consideration

276 *ADF* (n 7) [183].

277 Ibid., [183], [185].

278 *Merrill & Ring* (n 7) [211] (emphasis added).

279 For a critical analysis of the award, see Dumberry (n 2) 115–117.

> of inappropriate behavior of a sort, which while difficult to define, may still be regarded as unfair, inequitable or unreasonable.[280]

The *Cargill* Tribunal adopted a much more cautious approach. First, it stated that it is 'widely accepted that extensive adoption of identical treaty language by many States may in and of itself serve – again with care – as evidence of customary international law.'[281] The Tribunal mentioned the fact that FET clauses were widespread in BITs, but also noted that their actual language varies. For this reason, it held that 'significant evidentiary weight should not be afforded to autonomous clauses inasmuch as it could be assumed that such clauses were adopted precisely because they set a standard other than that required by custom.'[282] The Tribunal concluded that it did not 'believe it prudent to accord significant weight to even widespread adoption of such [FET] clauses.'[283] It also added that: 'It may be that widespread adoption of a strict autonomous meaning to "fair and equitable treatment" may in time raise international expectations as to what constitutes good governance, but such a consequence is different than such clauses evidencing directly an evolution of custom.'[284]

In sum, only two awards (*Pope & Talbot*, and *Merrill & Ring*) have clearly adopted the position that the FET standard has become a rule of custom, while the reasoning of another (*Mondev*) may also be interpreted as such an endorsement. It should be added that there are some other awards which contain some rather vague reference which could be considered as somehow also supporting this proposition.[285]

The next section examines concretely how a treaty-based norm can transform into a customary rule.

3 *Assessing the Customary Status of the FET Standard*

This section will concretely assess the controversial proposition recognising the customary status of the FET standard.[286] I will first briefly explain

280 Ibid., [210].
281 *Cargill* (n 7) [276].
282 Ibid.
283 Ibid.
284 Ibid.
285 For instance, in *Blusun* (n 181) [319(3)], the Tribunal concluded that Article 10 ECT 'incorporates the fair and equitable treatment standard *under customary international law* and as applied by tribunals' (emphasis added).
286 For a comprehensive analysis of the question, see: Dumberry (n 3) 159ff.

the phenomenon of custom in the specific context of investment arbitration (Section 3.1.). I will also examine the question of how (and under which conditions) provisions contained in BITs can transform into customary rules (Section 3.2.). I will then examine the practice of States to include FET clauses in their BITs and determine whether it is general and widespread, representative and uniform and consistent (Section 3.3.). Finally, I will address the question of whether or not these States have any *opinio juris* with respect to the FET standard (Section 3.4.).

3.1 Introductory Remarks on the Phenomenon of Custom

Although it has been criticized for being unsatisfactory, the starting point of any analysis on custom is Article 38(1) of the Statute of the ICJ.[287] The provision enumerates a (non-exhaustive[288]) list of the formal 'sources of international law', one of which is 'international custom.' Article 38 uses the following (rather awkward) wording: 'international custom, as evidence of a general practice accepted as law.'[289] Investor-State arbitration tribunals frequently refer to Article 38 as an authoritative statement of the sources of international law.[290] In the present author's view, any enquiry into the sources of international *investment* law must be based on the recognized sources of *general* international law listed under this provision. This is because investment arbitration is part

287 *Statute of the ICJ*, reprinted in International Court of Justice, Charter of the United Nations, Statute and Rules of Court and other Documents 61 (No. 4 1978).

288 J. d'Aspremont, *Formalism and the Sources of International Law* (Oxford UP 2011) 149.

289 As rightly noted by Mark E. Villiger, *Customary International law and Treaties: A Manual on the Theory and Practice of the Interrelation of Sources* (2nd edn., Kluwer 1997) 15, 'the Court cannot apply a custom, [but] only customary law', and it is in fact the 'general practice accepted as law which constitutes evidence of a customary rule' not the other way around. A better definition of custom is the one adopted by ILC Special Rapporteur Wood in his Second Report (International Law Commission, 'Second Report on Identification of Customary International Law', by Michael Wood, Special Rapporteur, Sixty-sixth session, Geneva, 5 May–6 June and 7 July–8 August 2014, UN Doc. A/CN.4/672 [hereinafter referred to as ILC, Second Report, 2014], Draft Conclusion 2 of the ILC 'Proposed draft conclusions on the identification of customary international law'): customary international law 'means those rules of international law that derive from and reflect a general practice accepted as law'.

290 See, the analysis in: Dumberry (n 3) 30ff. I have found no award rejecting the relevance of Article 38.

of public international law.[291] It is not a self-contained regime.[292] However, as mentioned by Tams, reference to Article 38 can only be the *starting point* of any enquiry about the sources of international *investment* law.[293] A recent book on the sources of rights and obligations in international investment law includes chapters on *other* sources, including State contracts and national laws.[294]

As explained by ILC Special Rapporteur Wood, the so-called 'double requirement' under Article 38 (State practice and *opinio juris*) is 'generally adopted in the practice of States and the decisions of international courts and tribunals, including the [ICJ]' and it is 'widely endorsed in the literature.'[295] The double requirement is often referred to as the 'traditional' approach.[296] A number of scholars have rejected this approach and instead developed alternative theories generally focusing on the prevalence of *opinio juris* rather than actual State practice.[297]

The present author has adopted the 'traditional' approach whereby *both* State practice and *opinio juris* must be demonstrated.[298] As summarized by one

---

291 C. Tams, 'The Sources of International Investment Law' in T. Gazzini and E. de Brabandere (eds.), *International Investment Law: The Sources of Rights and Obligations* (Martinus Nijhoff 2012) 320; M. Forteau, 'La contribution au développement du droit international général de la jurisprudence arbitrale relative aux investissements étrangers', (2009) 4(1) Ann. Brasileiro DI, 14; Alvarez (n 73) 76; McLachlan et al. (n 82) 15; Claire Crepet Daigremont, 'Les sources du droit international des investissements', in C. Leben (ed) *Droit international des investissements et l'arbitrage transnational* (Pedone 2015) 84.

292 *Archer Daniels Midland Company and Tate and Lyle Ingredients Americas, Inc., v. Mexico*, ICSID Case No. ARB(AF)/04/05, Award, 21 November 2007 [195].

293 Tams (n 291) 319.

294 Gazzini and De Brabandere (n 16).

295 ILC Second Report (n 289) 8.

296 In a recent article, A.E. Roberts, 'Traditional and Modern Approaches to Customary International Law: A Reconciliation', (2001) 95 AJIL, 758, notably described this approach as one 'focus[ing] primarily on state practice in the form of interstate interaction and acquiescence', with *opinio juris* being 'a secondary consideration invoked to distinguish between legal and nonlegal obligations'.

297 These theories are examined in detail in: Dumberry (n 3). See also, the analysis in: ILC, First Report, 2013 (n 151) 47ff.

298 Dumberry (n 3) 30ff. As noted by one writer (Maurice H. Mendelson, 'The Formation of Customary International Law' (1985) 192 Rec. des cours, 372), these alternative theories have 'received virtually no support in the practice of States or in the case-law' (with the exception of a few decisions of the International Tribunal for the Former Yugoslavia (ICTY), including *Prosecutor v. Kupreškić*, ICTY Case No. IT-95–16-T (ICTY Trial Chamber), 14 January 2000 [527]).

writer, 'the reason why both elements can be seen to be necessary is that without *usus* it would not be customary and without *opinio* it would not be law.'[299] On the one hand, custom simply cannot be created by mere *opinio juris*, without any State practice backing such a belief.[300] Thus, deducing custom 'purely from *opinio juris* can create utopian laws that cannot regulate reality.'[301] Put differently, *opinio juris* without State practice is 'nothing more than rhetoric.'[302] On the other hand, it is necessary to demonstrate *opinio juris* for two reasons. First, it is essential in distinguishing between real international law obligations and conduct that is merely based on other *non-legal* motivations,[303] such as 'courtesy, political expediency, will or compromise, precautionary measures, expressions of intent and aspirations or preferences'.[304] This essential distinction has been recognized by the ICJ.[305] Second, demonstrating *opinio juris* is necessary to explain how the accumulation of uniform and consistent State practice can 'transform' into a legal rule *binding* on all States.[306] As noted by the ICJ in the *North Sea Continental Shelf* cases, 'acting, or agreeing to act in a certain way, does not itself demonstrate anything of a juridical nature.'[307] It is indeed fundamental to be able to explain how something that States *often and typically do* becomes something that they *feel they have to do* under

299 Jörg Kammerhofer, 'Customary International Law Needs both *Opinio* and *Usus*', paper presented at the conference 'The Role of *Opinio Juris* in Customary International Law', Duke-Geneva Institute in Transnational Law, Geneva, 2013, 2.

300 Villiger (n 289), 288; H.W.A. Thirlway, *International Customary Law and Codification* (Sijthoff 1972) 56.

301 Roberts (n 296) 757.

302 Y. Dinstein, 'The Interaction between Customary International Law and Treaties', (2006) 322 Rec. des cours, 294.

303 Villiger (n 289) 48.

304 International Law Commission, 'Formation and Evidence of Customary International Law, Elements in the Previous Work of the ILC that Could be Particularly Relevant to the Topic', Memorandum by the Secretariat, Sixty-fifth session Geneva, 5 May–7 June and 8 July–9 August 2013, UN Doc., A/CN.4/659 [hereinafter referred to as ILC, Memorandum, 2013] 19.

305 *Colombian-Peruvian Asylum Case*, Judgment, ICJ Rep. 1950, 285, 286; *North Sea Continental Shelf Cases* (n 19) 44 [77]. See also: ILC Second Report (n 289) 42–43, listing a number of individual opinions of ICJ judges.

306 Karol Wolfke, *Custom in Present International Law* (2nd ed., Nijhoff 1993) 44.

307 *North Sea Continental Shelf Cases* (n 19) 44 [76].

international law.[308] In the words of Dinstein, *opinio juris* 'underpins the transition of State practice from the normal to the normative.'[309]

In any event, this double requirement has been recognized by *all* investment tribunals which have explained the concept of custom.[310] Moreover, States recognize this double requirement in their pleadings in arbitration proceedings as well as in recent investment treaties.[311] In fact, I have found no example of State practice where a State has rejected the necessity to demonstrate both elements of custom.

A few words, should be said about arbitral awards and the phenomenon of the creation of custom.[312] Awards are not a formal source of international law and therefore cannot be considered as evidence of *State* practice for the formation of customary rules. Yet, while international judges or arbitrators have no formal role in the creation of these rules, they nevertheless play an essential role in 'revealing' their existence as well as in their development and evolution. Thus, any decision/award containing a comprehensive and persuasive analysis (based on a detailed examination of both State practice and *opinio juris*) on whether or not a given rule should be considered as custom will greatly influence other future tribunals as well as the subsequent practice of States. The *Windstream* Tribunal has recently referred to the role of awards as 'indirect evidence' to determine the content of custom.[313] Yet, in my book I observed

---

308 International Law Commission, 'Third Report on Identification of Customary International Law', by Michael Wood, Special Rapporteur, Sixty-seventh session, Geneva, 4 May–5 June and 6 July–7 August 2014, A/CN.4/682 [hereinafter referred to as ILC, Third Report, 2015] 6.

309 Dinstein (n 302) 294. See also: ILC Second Report (n 289) 41.

310 *Cambodia Power Company v. Cambodia and Electricité du Cambodge LLC*, ICSID Case No. ARB/09/18, Decision on Jurisdiction, 22 March 2011 [333]; *Daimler Financial Servcies AG v. Argentina*, ICSID Case No. ARB/05/1, Award, 22 August 2012 [622, 310]; *Glamis* (n 7) [602]; *MCI Power* (n 6) [369]; *Mobil* (n 15) [127]; *El Paso* (n 6) [622]; *Merrill & Ring* (n 42) [193, 204, 201]; *Railroad* (n 6) [216]; *Apotex* (n 7) [9.25]; *UPS* (n 149) [84]; *Windstream* (n 7) [351]; Cargill (n 7) [274]; *EnCana Corporation v. Ecuador*, LCIA Case No. UN 3481, Award, 3 February 2006 [147]; *Teinver* (n 10) [666].

311 See, the analysis in: Dumberry (n 3) 35ff.

312 On this question, see: Dumberry (n 3), 283ff; Patrick Dumberry, 'The Role and Relevance of Awards in the Formation, Identification and Evolution of Customary Rules in International Investment Law', (2016) 33(3) J Int. Arb.

313 *Windstream* (n 7) 351 ('in principle the content of a rule of customary international law such as the minimum standard of treatment can best be determined on the basis of evidence of actual State practice establishing custom that also shows that the States have accepted such practice as law (*opinio juris*). However, the Tribunal notes that neither Party has produced such evidence in this arbitration. In the circumstances, the Tribunal must

that arbitral tribunals have so far generally failed in their task of properly revealing the existence of customary rules.[314] Thus, instead of conducting their *own* analysis of practice and *opinio juris*, they generally simply rely on the findings of other tribunals.[315]

In my view,[316] customary rules of international investment law remain of fundamental importance today even in light of the present proliferation of BITs.[317] For one thing, the MST and the general prohibition against expropriation without compensation can now be considered as well-established customary rules.[318] The very existence of these rules is a testament to the continuing importance of custom. Custom is also relevant for three reasons. First, custom is the applicable legal regime of protection in the absence of any BIT. Second, custom is, of course, also important in the many instances where BITs make explicit reference to the concept. Third, custom plays a gap-filling role whenever a treaty, a contract or domestic legislation is silent on a given issue. Finally, in my view, arbitral tribunals should *always* take into account relevant rules of customary international law for the simple reason that 'international law' is the applicable law in the overwhelming majority of arbitration disputes.[319]

3.2 How Can Provisions Contained in BITs Transform into Customary Rules?

Having briefly exposed the phenomenon of custom, this section explains how treaty-based norms can transform into customary rules.[320] While custom and treaties are two distinct sources of international law, they remain in many

---

rely on other, indirect evidence in order to ascertain the content of the customary international law minimum standard of treatment; the Tribunal cannot simply declare *non liquet*. Such indirect evidence includes, in the Tribunal's view, decisions taken by other NAFTA tribunals that specifically address the issue of interpretation and application of Article 1105(1) of NAFTA, as well as relevant legal scholarship'), See also, 358.

314 See, Dumberry (n 3), 283ff.

315 One rare exception is *UPS* (n 149) [85ff].

316 See the analysis in: Dumberry (n 3), 351ff; Patrick Dumberry, 'A Few Observations on the Remaining Fundamental Importance of Customary Rules in the Age of Treatification of International Investment Law', (2016) 43(1) ASA Bull. 41–61.

317 Gazzini (n 11) 691. See also: Christoph H. Schreuer, Loretta Malintoppi, August Reinisch & Anthony Sinclair, *The ICSID Convention; A Commentary* (2nd ed Cambridge UP 2009) 606; M. Hirsch, 'Sources of International Investment Law', ILA Report (2011) 7–8; Alvarez (n 73) 74.

318 For a detailed analysis, see Dumberry (n 3) 92ff.

319 The issue is examined in detail in: Dumberry (n 3) 368ff.

320 The issue is examined in detail in: Dumberry (n 3) 172ff.

ways 'entangled.'[321] It is generally recognized that there are three forms of interactions between custom and treaties,[322] including the possibility for patterns of treaties containing the same (or very similar) provision to contribute to the formation of a *new* rule of customary international law in the future. The phenomenon is widely recognized by scholars,[323] by the work of the ILC[324] and the ILA,[325] and is also reflected at Article 38 of the *Vienna Convention on the Law of Treaties*. One important point to highlight is that while a treaty (or treaties) can be 'the historic (material) source of a customary rule,' it cannot be considered as the 'formal' source.[326] Thus, while treaties may be considered as the starting point of the eventual development of a new customary rule, the 'formal' source of the development of custom consists in the actual practice of States afterward.[327] Another closely related phenomenon is the so-called 'crystallisation' of custom.[328]

Most scholars agree that, in theory, the content of a series of *bilateral* treaties may contribute to the development of a new customary rule.[329] A number of writers have also taken the same position specifically regarding BITs.[330]

---

321 Oscar Schachter, 'Entangled Treaty and Custom' in Yoram Dinstein (ed), *International Law at a Time of Perplexity: Essays in Honour of Shabtai Rosenne* (Martinus Nijhoff 1989) 717–738; Maurice Mendelson, 'Disentangling Treaty and Customary International Law' (1987) 81 ASIL Proc. 157–163.

322 On this question, see Villiger (n 289) 195 ff.

323 R. Baxter, 'Treaties and Custom', (1970) 129 Rec. des cours, 57ff; Villiger (n 289) 167ff; Dinstein (n 302) 371ff; Al Faruque (n 71) 298–299.

324 ILC Memorandum (n 304) 33. A number of contemporary examples of such a phenomenon are examined in: ILC Third Report (n 308) 27.

325 International Law Association, 'Statement of Principles Applicable to the Formation of General Customary International Law', Final Report of the Committee on the Formation of Customary Law, Conference Report London (2000) 17 [hereinafter ILA, Final Report] 46.

326 Ibid., 46.

327 See Villiger (n 289) 26. The ICJ has recognized this important distinction: *Continental Shelf (Libyan Arab Jamahiriya/Malta)*, Judgment, ICJ Rep. 1985, 13, 29–30. See also: *North Sea Continental Shelf Cases* (n 19) 104, Separate Opinion of Judge Ammoun.

328 Here, the treaty is *not* the starting point of the eventual formation of a rule. The treaty intervenes later in the process by *boosting* pre-existing State practice and helping the crystallization of a slowly emerging new rule of custom. See, ILA Final Report (n 325) 49; *North Sea Continental Shelf Cases* (n 19) [63]; *Fisheries Jurisdiction Case* (United Kingdom v. Iceland), ICJ Rep. 1974 [51–52].

329 See, the list of writers in Dumberry (n 3) 174.

330 See, the list of writers in: Ibid. 175.

In fact, a number of tribunals have also acknowledged such a possibility.[331] Yet, there is certainly no presumption that a series of bilateral treaties will necessarily lead to said transformation.[332] Thus, the main reason why States ratify bilateral treaties in the first place is 'precisely because they believe that no customary rules exist, or will exist, on the matter.'[333] This is exactly what happened with BITs. States started to sign BITs *en masse* in the 1990s because there were strong disagreements amongst them regarding whether or not any customary rule existed at the time.[334] Thus, on the one hand developing (and socialist) States generally believed that no rule of customary international law had crystallised as a result of their opposition to such norms. On the other hand, developed States were of the opinion that while such customary rules existed, their effectiveness was limited as a result of the vehement opposition of a large number of States.

A basic question needs to be asked whenever assessing whether a treaty-based rule contained in a bilateral treaty can transform into a rule of custom.[335] In the words of the ICJ, a provision must be of a 'fundamentally norm-creating character such as could be regarded as forming the basis of a general rule of law.'[336] While for some writers, the FET standard has the potential to develop as a rule of custom,[337] others have pointed out to the fact that the FET standard 'is characterized by lack of clarity concerning the principle's normative content and scope' and that it 'does not have a precise content that can easily be applied.'[338] Surprisingly, this position is in fact taken by writers who argue

331 *Pope & Talbot* (n 155) [59]; *Cargill* (n 7) [276]; *Camuzzi International S.A. v. Argentina*, ICSID Case No. ARB/03/2, Decision on Jurisdiction, 11 May 2005 [144]; *Sempra* (n 6) [156]; *CME Czech Republic B.V. v. Czech Republic*, UNCITRAL, Final Award, 14 March 2003 [498]. The reasoning of a number of other tribunals also suggests (at least implicitly) that such a transformation is possible: *Glamis* (n 7) [603]; *UPS* (n 149) [86]; *Chemtura* (274) [121]; *ADF* (n 7) [183].

332 ILA Final Report (n 325) 47–48; Vasciannie (n 88) 158, fn 323; Wolfke (n 306) 69; McLachlan (n 81) 392.

333 Villiger (n 289) 189. Yet, one cannot simply deduce from the fact that States have entered into a treaty that they *necessarily* consider that no customary rules exist *at all*. There are indeed perfectly good reasons for States to sign a treaty and *at the same time* consider some *specific* provisions contained in that treaty as codifying existing custom.

334 Haeri (n 26) 43; Sornarajah (n 12) 19–20, 213–214.

335 See: d'Aspremont (n 16) 33–34.

336 *North Sea Continental Shelf Cases* (n 19) [72]. On this notion, see, Villiger (n 289) 177–178.

337 Vasciannie (n 88) 154.

338 ILA, 'General Public International Law and International Investment Law – A Research Sketch on Selected Issues', International Law Association German Branch Sub-Committee on Investment Law (2009) 10–11; Gazzini (n 11) 698; Faruque (n 71) 304.

that the FET standard is indeed a rule of custom. For instance, Tudor believes that 'given the flexibility of the notion and the ways in which it is adapted and applied to a case, the FET has no stable or fixed content.'[339] But one writer has rightly asked how a norm without fixed content can become a norm of customary international law.[340] For this reason, some writers have concluded that the FET standard simply cannot transform into a custom rule.[341]

In any event, there are two strict conditions that need to be fulfilled for a treaty-based rule to transform into a new rule of custom. First, it needs to be shown that a significant number of States have entered into numerous BITs that contain the same provision (or very similarly-drafted clauses). For the ICJ, what is required is that 'State practice, including that of States whose interest are specially affected, should [be] both extensive and virtually uniform in the sense of the provision invoked (...).[342] In other words, the practice of States who are *parties* to BITs must be uniform, consistent, and representative. Second, it needs to be shown that States (including those *not* party to these BITs) have also adopted in their own practice (outside the treaty) the type of conduct prescribed in these instruments. Thus, what matters is the existence of a consistent practice of States *outside* the treaty framework.[343] The next section examines concretely whether or not these two conditions are met regarding the practice of States to include FET clauses in their BITs.

3.3 Examination of State Practice

This section will first examine the practice of States that are parties to BITs containing FET clauses (Section 3.3.1.), which will then be followed by a brief analysis of the practice of States *outside* the BIT framework (Section 3.3.2.).

3.3.1 *The Practice of States Parties to BITs*

The first condition for a treaty-based norm, such as the FET standard, to transform into a customary rule concerns the practice of States that are *parties* to

339 Tudor (n 1) 133. See also: Ioana Knoll-Tudor, 'The Fair and Equitable Treatment Standard and Human Rights Norms' in P.M. Dupuy, F. Francioni and E.U. Petersmann (eds) *Human Rights in International Investment Law and Arbitration* (Oxford UP 2009), 317; Diehl (n 1) 135 ('it is the very nature of standard not to be uniform and specific but to be broad and open for fact-specific analysis').

340 S.W. Schill, book review of Tudor's work (2009) 20 EJIL, 237.

341 Orakhelashvili (n 275) 104; d'Aspremont (n 16) 24, 33–34; Gazzini (n 11) 698. See also: Paparinskis (n 1) 172.

342 *North Sea Continental Shelf Cases* (n 19) 43 [74]. See also: ILC Third Report (n 308) 26.

343 Dinstein (n 302) 376–377; Villiger (n 289) 183–184; R. Baxter, 'Multilateral Treaties as Evidence of Customary International Law', (1965–1966) 41 British YIL, 296–297.

BITs containing such a clause. Their practice must be not only general and widespread (Section 3.3.1.1.) amongst a largely representative number of States (Section 3.3.1.2.), but also uniform and consistent (Section 3.3.1.3.).[344]

3.3.1.1 State Practice is General and Widespread

In order for a customary rule to emerge, State practice must be general,[345] or in the words of the ICJ, 'widespread'[346] and 'sufficiently extensive and convincing.'[347] This is, however, a relative requirement. Thus, no 'precise number or percentage of States' is required to demonstrate general practice.[348] Also, whether or not a practice is widespread and extensive enough cannot be determined in the abstract; it will always depend on the circumstances. What matters is the degree of *representativeness* of the States actively engaged in that practice.[349]

The inclusion of FET clauses in modern BITs is general and widespread. As noted above, I have examined close to 2,000 BITs and found that only 50 of them did not include any FET clause and that 25 others referred to the standard only in their preambles. Thus, less than five per cent of all BITs examined do not include any formal and binding FET obligation for the host State of investments. Although a few BITs contain slightly different language than the expression FET *per se*,[350] not so much weight should be given to these variations

344 Gazzini (n 11) 701.

345 ILC Memorandum (n 304) 10–11 (noting the different expressions used by the ILC); ILC Second Report (n 289) 34; Al Faruque (n 71) 296.

346 *Maritime Delimitation and Territorial Questions between Qatar and Bahrain*, Merits, Judgment, ICJ Rep. 2001, 40, 102 [205]; *Fisheries Jurisdiction Case* (n 89) 45, 52 (Joint Separate Opinion of Judges Forster, Bengzon, Jiménez de Aréchaga, Nagendra Singh and Ruda).

347 *Delimitation of the Maritime Boundary in the Gulf of Maine Area* (*Canada/United States*), Judgment, ICJ Rep. 1984, 299 [111].

348 Mendelson (n 298), 219–224.

349 ILA Final Report (n 325) 25, 26; ILC Second Report (n 289) 34.

350 Thus, I have found 12 BITs which only refer to 'fair' treatment, including 9 BITs entered into by Iran and 3 by Russia. Also, 5 BITs referred to the expression 'just and fair' and 13 only to 'equitable' treatment, including 7 entered into by China and 4 by Malaysia. Finally, 8 BITs referred to 'just and equitable' treatment (including 3 by Germany) and 12 others to the term 'equitable and reasonable' (including 3 by Italy, 6 by Norway, and 3 by the Philippines).

of language.[351] The following table shows which States have entered into BITs containing no FET clause:[352]

State	Number of BITs with no FET clause (out of the total number of BITs entered into by that State)	Name of the other States party to these BITs without FET clause
Romania	7 (82)	Senegal, Albania, Cameroon, Denmark, Egypt, Ghana, Pakistan
Germany	8 (134)	Iran, Liberia, Malaysia, Niger, Rwanda, Senegal, Singapore, Togo
Japan	7 (22)	Mongolia, Pakistan, Sri Lanka, Turkey, Bangladesh, China, Egypt
Egypt	5 (100)	Georgia, Japan, Romania, US, Albania
Albania	4 (43)	Croatia, Egypt, Greece, Romania
Turkey	5 + 21 others with FET only in the preamble (89)	Bulgaria, China, Indonesia, Japan, Kazakhstan + Algeria, Albania, Bosnia, Croatia, Cuba, Egypt, India, Jordan, Kazakhstan, Kyrgyzstan, Latvia, Malta, Moldova, Pakistan, Qatar, South Africa, Sudan, Tajikistan, Turkmenistan, China, Tunisia
Senegal	4 (26)	Germany, Netherlands, Romania, Sweden
Bulgaria	4 (68)	Cyprus, Malta, Sweden, Turkey
China	3 (130)	Japan, Slovakia, Turkey
Italy	3 (92)	Malta, Albania, Algeria
Malta	3 (21)	Libya (not in force), Bulgaria, Italy
Pakistan	3 (46)	Japan, Philippines, Romania

351 See, the discussion in Dumberry (n 2) 58. See also: *Luigiterzo Bosca v. Lithuania*, PCA case no. 2011-05, 17 May 2013 [196]; *Total* (n 10) [125, 106].

352 It should be added that a number of States have 2 BITs each with no FET clause: Greece, France, Philippines, Croatia, Sweden, Czech Republic, Indonesia. The following States have only one such BIT: Belgium, Cyprus, Cameroon, Georgia, Ghana, Korea, Iran, Liberia, Libya, Madagascar, Mongolia, Netherlands, Niger, Rwanda, Slovakia, Singapore, Bangladesh, Togo, Tunisia, United Kingdom, Ukraine, United States, Denmark, Indonesia.

A few observations can be made about those few BITs containing no FET obligations. First, no State has systematically excluded FET clauses from its treaties. The few States which have omitted such clauses more often than others have only done so in a minority of their BITs. Second, one third of all Japanese and Turkish BITs do not include any binding FET clause. These Japanese BITs have all been entered into with developing States. However, Turkey has entered into those BITs (with no FET clause) with both developing and developed States (all from Eastern Europe and the former USSR, except for Japan). These features suggest that both States may have insisted during treaty negotiation for excluding the presence of any FET clause. Not surprisingly, the Japan-Turkey BIT does not include such a clause. Third, about 10% of all Romanian, Albanian, Greek, and Senegalese BITs have no FET clauses. The majority of such Romanian BITs have been entered into with developing States. All Greek BITs (that do not contain an FET clause) have been signed with States from Eastern Europe and the former USSR. The same is true for most Albanian BITs. Not surprisingly, the BITs entered into between these three States (Albania-Greece BIT, Albania-Romania BIT) also do not include an FET clause. These patterns suggest that the absence of an FET clause may have been an important aspect for these States during treaty negotiation. Overall, it seems that BITs with no FET clauses have been more popular in Eastern Europe than elsewhere. In general (with the exception of Japan), such clauses are not favoured by developing States. Only Germany has adopted such clause in nine of its 134 BITs, all with developing States (except for the one signed with Romania).

In sum, the practice of States to include FET clauses in their BITs is general and widespread.

3.3.1.2 State Practice is Representative

The representativeness of the practice of States is another key aspect when assessing the customary nature of a provision contained in treaties. Thus, for the ILA, 'it is not simply a question of how many States participate in the practice, but *which* States.'[353] The ICJ in the *North Sea Continental Shelf* cases also speaks of 'very widespread and *representative* participation' in the development of a rule.[354] Different (but not necessarily conflicting) interpretations as to what representativeness actually means have been put forward. For some,

353 ILA Final Report (n 325) 25 (emphasis in the original).

354 *North Sea Continental Shelf Cases* (n 19) [73] (emphasis added).

a representative practice means that it includes those States from 'all major political and social-economic systems.'[355] What matters, to quote the ICJ in the *North Sea Continental Shelf* cases,[356] is the practice of those 'specially affected' States.[357] Which States are 'specially affected' will vary depending on the circumstances.[358]

While the FET standard was first developed by Western States to provide protection to their companies when investing in developing countries,[359] it remains that today it has also been embraced by developing States.[360] Thus, the standard was included in regional multilateral instruments related to the protection of foreign investments not only in Europe (Energy Charter Treaty) and in North America (NAFTA) but also in Latin America[361] Asia[362] and Africa[363] and in model BITs of developing States. FET clauses have also been included in BITs entered into between developing countries.[364] As mentioned above, my own investigation shows no clear pattern of a specific group of States systematically rejecting the FET clause.

In sum, the practice of States to include FET clauses in their BITs can be considered as representative.

---

355 Villiger (n 289) 29; Brigitte Stern, 'Custom at the Heart of International Law' (2001) 11 Duke JCIL, 105. This is, for instance, the position taken by Judge Lachs in his dissenting opinion in the *North Sea Continental Shelf Cases* (n 19) 227.

356 Ibid. [73]. See also: Ibid [175–6] (dissenting opinion of Judge Tanaka); *Fisheries Jurisdiction Case* (n 89) 90 (separate opinion of Judge De Castro), 161 (separate opinion of Judge Petrén).

357 *North Sea Continental Shelf Cases* (n 19) [73–74].

358 ILA Final Report (n 325) 26; See also: Baxter, (n 323) 66; Dinstein (n 302) 289; ILC Second Report (n 289) 36.

359 This is clear from the inclusion of these clauses in early drafting attempts, such as the 1959 *Draft Convention on Investments Abroad* (n 93) and the 1967 OECD *Draft Convention* (n 76) 11, both reflecting the position of developing States.

360 See, for instance: OECD, *International Investment Law: A Changing Landscape, A Companion Volume to International Investment Perspectives* (2005) 78; OECD (n 22) 5.

361 Art. 2, *Colonia Protocol* in the context of Mercosur.

362 *ASEAN Treaty for the Promotion and Protection of Investments* (Article IV).

363 *Common Market for Eastern and Southern Africa* (COMESA) (Article 159(1)a).

364 Vasciannie (n 88) 129–130.

3.3.1.3 State Practice is Not Uniform and Consistent

According to several ICJ cases,[365] the practice of States must be 'uniform' and consistent.[366] The ILA speaks of the requirement of 'virtual uniformity'[367] both 'internally'[368] and 'collectively'.[369] Collective uniformity requires that 'different States must not have engaged in substantially different conduct, some doing one thing and some another.'[370] Thus, as noted by the ILA, 'if there is too much inconsistency between States in their practice, there is no *general* custom and hence no general customary rule.'[371] This requirement has been recognized by States in arbitration proceedings[372] as well as by investment tribunals.[373]

Is the practice of States to include FET clauses in their BITs uniform and consistent? While admitting that 'BITs do not refer to the FET in a uniform manner,'[374] Tudor argues that there is enough uniformity in State practice for the emergence of a customary rule because the language differences contained in FET clauses 'refer to the level of the treatment to be accorded to the Investors, not to the standard within its content.'[375] Another writer has also recently argued that these drafting differences 'do not touch upon the core of the FET standard.'[376] The first obvious criticism put forward by other

365 *Asylum Case* (n 305), 276; *Military and Paramilitary Activities in and around Nicaragua,* (Nicaragua v. United States) Merits, Judgment, ICJ Rep. 1986, [186]; *Fisheries Jurisdiction Case* (n 89) 50 (Joint Separate Opinion of Judges Forster, Bengzon, Jiménez de Aréchaga, Nagendra Singh and Ruda).

366 See, Cai Congyan, 'International Investment Treaties and the Formation, Application and Transformation of Customary International Law Rules', (2008) 7 Chinese JIL 660; Al Faruque (n 71) 295–296; Gazzini (n 11) 692.

367 *North Sea Continental Shelf Cases* (n 19) [74].

368 ILA Final Report (n 325) 21, explaining that 'internal uniformity means that each State whose behaviour is being considered should have acted in the same way on virtually all of the occasions on which it engaged in the practice in question'.

369 ILA Final Report (n 325) 21. Mendelson (n 298) 212.

370 ILA Final Report (n 325) 21.

371 Ibid., 22 (emphasis in the original). Yet, as the ICJ recognized in *Nicaragua* (n 365) [186], in practical terms, it would be almost impossible for a rule of custom to ever emerge if *perfect and total* 'collective' consistency and uniformity was required amongst States.

372 *Glamis* (n 7) [602]; *Apotex* (n 7) [2.65]; *Mobil* (n 15) [131].

373 *Glamis* (n 7) [603]; *Merrill & Ring* (n 42) [204].

374 Tudor (n 1) 77.

375 Ibid.

376 Diehl (n 1) 134–5, adding that it 'is the very nature of standard not to be uniform and specific but to be broad and open for fact-specific analysis. If this particularity of the notion of standard constituted a bar to the formation of custom, then no standard of treatment could ever become part of customary international law.'

scholars[377] on this point is whether one can truly speak of 'uniformity' when there exists five or six different FET models.

As mentioned above, the most important drafting distinction lies between the following two groups of provisions: clauses explicitly linking the FET to the standard existing under international law, and others containing an unqualified formulation of the FET obligation. As noted above, the different language contained in these two types of FET clauses actually means *different things*.[378] As explained elsewhere by the present author[379] (and already mentioned above), drafting variations in FET clauses have been interpreted by arbitral tribunals to mean different content as well as different thresholds of liability.

In conclusion, while the practice of States to include FET clauses in their BITs is clearly general and widespread as well as representative, it remains that, in my view, such practice is not uniform enough for the standard to be considered as having emerged as a customary rule.[380] As a result, the first condition for any treaty-based norm to transform into a customary rule has not been met. In the next section, I will briefly examine whether the second condition has been fulfilled.

3.3.2 *The Practice of States outside the Treaty Framework*

While the first condition for the transformation of a treaty-based provision into a customary rule concerns the practice of States that are *parties* to BITs containing FET clauses, the second one deals with the practice of States *outside* the treaty framework. It must be shown that States have adopted 'a practice in-line with that prescribed (or authorized) by the treaty, but which is in fact independent of it because of the general rule that treaties neither bind nor benefit third parties.'[381] In other words, it must be demonstrated that States are actually uniformly and consistently providing the FET protection to foreign investors in their own practice *outside* treaties. For instance, the fact that States that are not party to any such BITs (or States parties to BITs not containing

377 Newcombe & Paradell (n 11) 271, fn 188; Congyan (366) 664, 667; Al Faruque (n 71) 304; Gazzini (n 11) 698; Bronfman (n 11) 656; Orakhelashvili (n 275) 77.

378 Surprisingly, Tudor (n 339) 316, who is supporting the customary status of the FET standard, admits that 'the *level of treatment* and the *exact meaning* of the FET depend on the wording of each clause' (emphasis added).

379 Dumberry (n 2) 40ff.

380 Moreover, the 'internal' practice of States regarding the use of the FET clause is nowhere near uniform either. A number of States (for instance, Mexico and Argentina) include different variations of FET clauses in their BITs.

381 ILA Final Report (n 325) 46. See also: Mendelson (n 298) 316; Villiger (n 289) 182–184; Dinstein (n 302) 376–377.

any FET clause) are doing so would be particularly convincing evidence of the customary nature of the FET obligation. Such practice could be found, for instance, in the domestic legislation of the host State.[382]

Some writers have suggested that the FET standard is found in the domestic laws of most developed and developing States.[383] An in-depth investigation of all domestic legal orders is clearly beyond the scope of this book. It suffices to say that one study of the domestic legislations of a number of capital-importing States by Vasciannie shows that the 'overwhelming majority' of these States do *not* provide FET protection to foreign investors.[384] Similarly, in a 1992 study of national legislations in 51 developing countries, Parra found that only three of them incorporated the FET standard.[385]

The present author has examined elsewhere the content of domestic laws dealing *specifically* with foreign investment laws.[386] These foreign investment laws (often referred to as 'code of investments') are of great importance in terms of investment protection. Thus, as noted by one writer, such legislation is 'normally a country's most authoritative, complete, and detailed statement of government policy toward foreign investment' and is in fact 'often the only statement of policy readily available to the investor, as well as to government officials with whom the investor must deal.'[387] I have examined 165 foreign investment laws (from 160 States).[388] Some preliminary observations should be made at the outset. First, a number of States do not have any specific domestic

---

382 It is generally recognized (see, for instance, ILC Second Report (n 289) 23) that acts of the legislative branch of government are manifestations of State practice which can potentially play a fundamental role in the emergence of customary rules. A number of international tribunals have recognized this phenomenon: *Nottebohm case (Liechtenstein v. Guatemala) (Second Phase)*, Judgment, ICJ Rep. 1955, 22; *Case Concerning the Arrest Warrant of 11 April 2000 (Democratic Republic of the Congo v. Belgium)*, Judgment, ICJ Rep. 2002, 24. The question is examined in detail in Dumberry (n 3) 268.

383 Tudor (n 1) 104 ('In the case of the FET standard, the situation as it stands today is that most developed and developing countries do recognize in their domestic laws that FET is to be applied to foreign investors. This is the case even though the term FET itself may not be employed as such but the content of FET, namely procedural and substantive guarantees for foreign investors, is found in national provisions'); Diehl (n 1) 174.

384 Vasciannie (n 88) 160.

385 A. Parra, 'Principles Governing Foreign Investment, as Reflected in National Investment Codes' (1992) 7 ICSID Rev. 435–7.

386 See, Dumberry (n 250).

387 Salacuse (n 77) 91.

388 I have conducted a survey of all investment laws contained in the World Bank's *Investment Laws of the World* compilation, which is updated twice a year. The compilation contained a significant number of the investment laws, but not all of them. Some investment laws

laws on foreign investment (which does not mean that investors get no legal protection at all when they make an investment in these countries). Second, a large number of existing foreign investment laws that I have examined (59) did not contain any specific provisions dealing with substantive investment protection. This is, for instance, the case of Canada's *Investment Act, 1985*. Again, not much can be deducted from that simple fact.[389]

Out of the 165 laws examined, I have found that only a few of them (10) expressly refer to the FET standard. While a number of these clauses are basic stand-alone FET provisions,[390] others are linked to the standard of protection existing under 'international law.'[391] One variant of the latter type of clause is a so-called 'no less' FET clause whereby international law is referred to as a threshold for the level of treatment to be accorded to foreign investors.[392] I have found another 'no less' clause where the threshold it set against 'international treaties' signed by that State, not international law per se.[393] In another clause, the law refers to the standard of protection existing under 'international law', without, however, using the words FET.[394] Finally, the drafting of another FET clause suggests that the State considers it has an obligation to provide this standard of protection to investors under international law.[395] The most explicit FET clause was found in Angola's *Private Investment Law* which specifically lists the types of protection which are covered by the provision.[396] It should be added that a number of other laws contain some much vaguer

were also retrieved online through official government websites or, in the alternative, through general online search engines.

389 In fact, legal protections for foreign investors making an investment in Canada are found elsewhere in Canada's legislation: J. Anthony VanDuzer, 'Report on Canada', in: Wenhua Shan (ed), *The Legal Protection of Foreign Investment*, (Hart Publi. 2012) 195, noting that 'Canada has not enacted specific legislation to give effect to its international investment obligations but takes the position that its domestic regime is consistent with its international obligations, including the standards for investor protection'.

390 Bangladesh, *Foreign Private Investment (Promotion and Protection) Act 1980*, Art. 4; Cape Verde, *External Investment Code, 1993*, Art. 7(1).

391 Democratic Republic of the Congo, *Code des investissements*, Art. 25; Venezuela, *Decree No 356 on Promotion and Protection of Investments, 1999*, Art. 6.

392 Kosovo, *Foreign Investment Law, 2014*, Art. 3(1).

393 Uzbekistan, *Law on Foreign Investments, 1998*, Art. 9.

394 Albania, *Law on Foreign Investments*, Art. 2(3). See also: Albanian Law No 7764 of 2 November 1993 on Foreign Investments, Art. 2(2).

395 Equatorial Guinea, *Ley de Regimen de Inversiones, 2001*, Art. 12: 'In conformity with its public international law obligations, the State commits to a fair and equitable treatment for all investors in its national territory.' (author's own translation).

396 Angola, *Private Investment Law*, Art. 15.

reference to the host State's obligation to apply the law 'equitably' to foreign investors and the rule of law,[397] and 14 laws contain references to a 'transparency' obligation.

In sum, only a handful of investment laws contain a reference to the FET standard. Yet, one has to be careful in drawing any conclusions from the fact that one State's domestic legislation does not include any FET protection. Just because such standard is not mentioned expressly in a State's foreign investment legislation *per se*, one cannot automatically conclude that it is absent from its domestic legal order. The standard may very well exist under that State's constitution.[398] Conversely, the fact that another State's legislation provides for such protection is no guarantee that investors actually receive FET treatment.

I have also analysed the question of whether or not State contracts entered into between States and companies (and individuals) contain FET clauses.[399] I have not found any contract referring to the standard. I have also found no arbitration award mentioning the presence of an FET clause in a contract and no case where a claimant has alleged the existence of any such FET obligation to be respected by the host State under a State contract. More generally, no arbitration case was found where a tribunal held that such an FET obligation exists in a situation of a BIT containing no FET clause or in the absence of any BIT.[400]

In sum, I have found no indicia in foreign investment laws (or contracts) supporting the conclusion that States are uniformly and consistently providing FET protection to foreign investors *outside* BITs. The second condition for the transformation of treaty-based provision into customary rule has therefore

397 Chad, *Loi instituant la Charte des investissements*, Art. 7; Gabon, *Charte des investissements*; Cameroon, *Law to Institute the Investment Charter*, Art. 8(1); Zimbabwe, *The Promotion of Investment: Policy and Regulations (1989)* [39]; Indonesia, *Law Concerning Investment*, Art. 3. See also: Art. 4(2)), 14.

398 Tudor (n 1) 104.

399 Dumberry (n 250). It is doubtful whether *confidential* State contracts can actually be considered as a relevant evidence of State practice. This is because of the publicity requirement whereby the practice that counts towards the formation of custom must be communicated to another State, or made public to a certain extent. See: Dumberry (n 3) 152.

400 It is true that in a handful of cases, foreign investors have been allowed to benefit from FET protection in situations where the BIT under which they started the proceedings did *not* contain any FET clause. Importantly, however, this was made possible through the use of the MFN clause contained in the BIT. Such importation of an FET protection had therefore nothing to do with the (alleged) customary status of the standard. On this question, see: Dumberry (n 255).

not been met. The next section will briefly examine the requirement of States' *opinio juris*.

3.4 Do States Have *opinio juris* When They include FET Clauses in Their BITS?

The existence of a rule of customary law does not only require that the practice of States be uniform, consistent, and representative, it must also be shown that States believe that they have an *obligation* under international law to provide FET protection to each other's investors *notwithstanding* the fact that such protection is set out in the BIT.[401] Thus, as explained by the ILC Special Rapporteur Wood, 'when the parties to a treaty act in fulfilment of their conventional obligations, this does not generally demonstrate the existence of an *opinio juris*.'[402] Thus, States simply fulfilling their treaty obligations has nothing to do with custom. As explained by Schachter, 'the repetition of common clauses in bilateral treaties does not create or support an inference that those clauses express customary law' because '[t]o sustain such a claim of custom one would have to show that *apart from the treaty itself*, the rules in the clauses *are considered obligatory*'.[403]

Considering the fact that Western States started including FET clauses in their BITS because of the ambiguities surrounding the concept of the MST, which was rejected by developing States, it would be, as noted by one writer, 'difficult to posit that there was consensus between developed and developing countries that the [FET] standard had passed into customary law,' adding that 'one would be hard-pressed to identify supportive *opinio juris*, particularly on the part of developing States.'[404] There is indeed no indication in treaty text (or in the *travaux preparatoires* or anywhere else) showing that States include FET clauses in their BITS out of a sense of conviction that this is the type of protection they *have* to provide to foreign investors *under international law*. While the present author has found a number of clear examples of such

401 In addition, it must also be shown that States have this belief outside the BIT framework. In other words, it must be demonstrated that they believe that they have an obligation under international law to provide FET protection to foreign investors despite having no formal treaty obligation to do so. See, ILC Second Report (n 289) 55.

402 ILC Second Report (n 289) 43, citing a number of individual opinions of ICJ judges. See also: *North Sea Continental Shelf Cases* (n 19) [76]; Dinstein (n 302) 299; Villiger (n 289) 26–27.

403 Oscar Schachter, 'Compensation for Expropriation' (1986) 78 AJIL 126 (emphasis added). See also: G.J.H. Van Hoof, *Rethinking the Sources of International Law* (Kluwer Law 1983) 109.

404 Vasciannie (n 88) 157–158.

existing *opinio juris* in BITs in other contexts,[405] none was found regarding the FET clause. States sign BITs to protect their own interests, not out of any sense of obligation.[406] They also include FET clauses in their BITs 'as a means of facilitating investment in their respective countries.'[407] In my recent book, I also discuss (and refute) the arguments invoked by a few scholars for whom States' *opinio juris* can simply be deduced from the fact that they have adopted numerous BITs containing FET provisions.[408]

4 *Conclusion*

The present chapter has argued that the FET standard should not be considered as a rule of customary international law. This is also the position adopted by a number of other scholars.[409] I have not found any evidence in treaties, pleadings or elsewhere of any State endorsing the controversial proposition about the customary status of FET which has been adopted by only two NAFTA tribunals (*Pope and Talbot* and *Merrill and Ring*). At the end of the day, the FET obligation remains a treaty-based standard of protection. There is therefore no legal basis for an investor to claim the general benefit of FET protection before an arbitral tribunal (which has jurisdiction over a given dispute) whenever the standard is not expressly mentioned in a treaty, the domestic law of the host State or in a State contract. This is indeed the conclusion reached by the Tribunal in the recent *Ickale* case:

---

405 See Dumberry (n 3) 325ff.

406 *UPS* (n 149) [97]: '[w]hile BITs are large in number, their coverage is limited (...) and in terms of *opinio juris* there is no indication that they reflect a general sense of obligation.' The same position has been adopted by many scholars: Guzman (n 60) 687; Carreau & Juillard (n 70) 469; Kirkman (n 244) 385; Vasciannie (n 88) 158–161; Bronfman (n 11) 670–671; Orakhelashvili (n 275) 77; Newcombe and Paradell (n 11) 270–271; Muchlinski (n 144) 701; Manu Sanan, 'International Investment Law; Questions Riddling an Answer' (2010) 2(1) Trade, Law and Development, 14; Haeri (n 26) 43; R. Doak Bishop, James Crawford & W. Michael Reisman, *Foreign Investment Disputes: Cases, Materials and Commentary* (Kluwer Law International 2005) 1065. See also, other reasons advanced by: Al Faruque (n 71) 310, 315; Congyan (n 366) 663, 665.

407 Haeri (n 26) 43.

408 Dumberry (n 3), 340 examining the position of Tudor (n 1) 80–84. See also: Diehl (n 1) 138, 145, 178 and Steffen Hindelang, 'Bilateral Investment Treaties, Custom and a Healthy Investment Climate – The Question of whether BITs Influence Customary International Law Revisited', (2004) 5 J. World Invest. & Trade, 795–796, 806, 808, for whom the existence of *opinio juris* is found in the concept of the 'general interests' of States.

409 Kirkman (n 244) 385; Norah Gallagher and Wenhua Shan, *Chinese Investment Treaties* (Oxford UP 2009) 127; Kill (n 11) 880; Al Faruque (n 71) 304; Orakhelashvili (n 275) 76 ff, 104; Vasciannie (n 88) 153 ff; Kläger (n 1) 268–270 (see however at 278).

> The Tribunal finds no merit, legal or otherwise, in the Claimant's argument that it is entitled to invoke the FET, FPS, non-discrimination, and umbrella clause protections on the basis that they have become "an international customary norm for Turkmenistan." In any event, even assuming the FET, FPS, non-discrimination, and umbrella clause standards were to be considered as part of customary international law (and not only the customary international law of, or applicable to, Turkmenistan), which is an argument neither Party has made, there is no basis in the BIT for the Tribunal to apply any investment protection standards other than those specifically included in the BIT. The State parties' consent to arbitrate in Article VII of the BIT only covers disputes arising out of an alleged breach of these specific standards.[410]

General Conclusion

This book has analysed the fascinating story of how the concept of the MST emerged in the early 20th Century, its decline for 30 years and finally its surprising recent 'resurrection' in the 2000s. The dynamic suddenly changed when arbitral tribunals started to give broad interpretation to FET clauses thereby providing foreign investors with treatment protections *above and beyond* the traditional MST. The importance given by these tribunals to the actual terms used in FET clauses lead States to start explicitly mentioning in their new BITs that the treatment offered to investors under these clauses was in fact the same treatment that existed to all foreign investors under the MST under custom. The concept of the MST, which had almost been forgotten by States in the 1990s, was now center stage in their quest to limit investor's rights under investment treaties. The very detailed FET clause contained in the CETA is the most vivid illustration of that recent trend.

It has been suggested that the FET clause should be abolished entirely in BITs precisely to 'reduce instances of creative interpretations by arbitral tribunals'.[411] Another question is whether the FET protection is in fact necessary at all in the context of a trade agreement between developed States that all promote economic liberalism and democracy. This is all the more questionable if one considers (as some scholars do[412]) that the FET standard contained

410 Ickale *Ickale* (n 255) [341].

411 Barrera (n 224) 1.

412 Schill (n 162); Vandevelde (n 162).

in BITs is in fact the equivalent of the rule of law found in the domestic legal orders of Canada and the member States of the EU.

Yet, for the time being the FET clause remains firmly present in the overwhelming majority of BITs. This is important given the fact that the FET obligation is a *treaty-based* standard of protection. It does not 'exist' outside the framework of an investment treaty (or potentially an investment law or a contract). Thus, the FET standard should not be considered as a rule of customary international law.

What are the concrete and practical consequences of my conclusion regarding the actual level of investment protection which host States must offer to foreign investors? First, my conclusion will have no consequence at all for investors protected by a BIT containing a FET clause. These (fortunate) investors are entitled to the FET protection provided for under the treaty notwithstanding the theoretical debate about the customary status of this obligation. Second, my conclusion will have limited practical impact for investors protected under the few BITs which contain no FET clause. This is the case for only about 5% of all BITs. Yet, these BITs will almost always contain a wide-scope MFN clause which will allow an investor to benefit from the FET protection contained in other treaties signed by the host State. In other words, these (less fortunate) investors will in most cases be able to get the FET protection existing elsewhere.

At the end of the day, my conclusion regarding the absence of customary status of the FET standard will have a very real and concrete impact only in the context where no BIT exists at all. Thus, an investor should not be allowed to claim the benefit of an FET protection under general international law. No such 'general' FET protection exists. It should be added, however, that all foreign investors (wherever they invest) can still claim the benefit of the MST under custom. The MST encompasses (at the very least) an obligation for host States to prevent the denial of justice in the administration of justice, to provide due process, to prevent arbitrary conduct, and to provide investors with 'full protection and security.'[413] In other words, foreign investors are allowed to benefit from important basic legal protections *even if* the FET standard is not deemed as a rule of custom.

413 Dumberry (n 2) 25–28.

Bibliography

Al Faruque, Abdullah, 'Creating Customary International Law Through Bilateral Investment Treaties: A Critical Appraisal' (2004) 44 Indian JIL 312–313.

Alvarez, Jose E., 'Bit on Custom' (2009–2010) 42 NYU J. Int'l L. & Pol.

d'Aspremont, Jean, 'International Customary Investment Law: Story of a Paradox' in T. Gazzini & E. de Brabandere (eds.), *International Investment Law: The Sources of Rights and Obligations* (Martinus Nijhoff 2012) 33.

Borchard, Edwin, 'The "Minimum Standard" of the Treatment of Aliens' (1939) 33 ASIL Proc. 55.

Blandford, Andrew C., 'The History of Fair and Equitable Treatment before the Second World War', (2017) 32(2) ICSID Rev.

Cai Congyan, 'International Investment Treaties and the Formation, Application and Transformation of Customary International Law Rules', (2008) 7 Chinese JIL.

Choudhury, Barnali, 'Evolution or Devolution? Defining Fair and Equitable Treatment in International Investment Law', (2005) 6(2) J. World Invest. & Trade.

Dickerson, Hollin, 'Minimum Standards', *Max Planck Encyclopedia of Public International Law* (Oxford: Oxford University Press, vol. 9, 2013).

Diehl, Alexandra, *The Core Standard of International Investment Protection: Fair and Equitable Treatment* (Wolters Kluwer 2012).

Dolzer R. & A. von Walter, 'Fair and Equitable Treatment – Lines of Jurisprudence on Customary Law' in F. Ortino (ed), *Investment Treaty Law, Current Issues II* (2007).

Dolzer, R., 'Fair and Equitable Treatment: A Key Standard in Investment Treaties', (2005) 39(1) Int'I Law, 360.

Dumberry, Patrick, *The Fair and Equitable Treatment Standard: A Guide to NAFTA Case Law on Article 1105* (Wolters Kluwer 2013).

Dumberry, Patrick, *The Formation and Identification of Rules of Customary International Law in International Investment Law* (Cambridge UP 2016).

Dumberry, Patrick, 'The Practice of States as Evidence of Custom: Fair and Equitable Treatment Standard Clauses in States' Foreign Investment Laws', (2015–16) 2 McGill JDR 66–81.

Dumberry, Patrick, 'Has the Fair and Equitable Treatment Standard become a Rule of Customary international Law?' (2017) 8(1) *Journal of International Dispute Settlement*, 155–178.

Dumberry, P. 'The 'Minimum Standard of Treatment' in International Investment Law: The Fascinating Story of the Emergence, the Decline and the Recent Resurrection of a Concept', in: Luca Pasquet, Klara Polackova Van der Ploeg, and Léon Castellanos Jankiewicz (eds), *International Law and Time: Narratives and Techniques: Proceedings of the conference International Law and Time* (Springer, 2018).

Dumberry, P., 'The Importation of the Fair and Equitable Treatment Standard Through MFN Clauses: An Empirical Study of BITS', (2016) 17 ICSID Rev. 229–259.

Dumberry, P., 'Shopping for a Better Deal: The Use of MFN Clauses to Get 'Better' Fair and Equitable Treatment Protection', (2016) Arb. Int. 1–16.

Dumberry, P., 'A Few Observations on the Remaining Fundamental Importance of Customary Rules in the Age of Treatification of International Investment Law', (2016) 43(1) ASA Bull. 41–61.

Dumberry, P., 'Fair and Equitable Treatment', in: Stefanie Schacherer & Makane Moïse Mbengue (eds), *Foreign Investment under the Comprehensive Economic and Trade Agreement (CETA)* (Springer 2018).

Gazzini, Tarcisio, 'The Role of Customary International Law in the Field of Foreign Investment' (2007) 8 Journal of World Investment and Trade.

Haeri, Hussein, 'A Tale of Two Standards: 'Fair and Equitable Treatment' and the Minimum Standard in International Law' (2011) 27 Arb. Int'l 31–32.

International Law Association, 'Statement of Principles Applicable to the Formation of General Customary International Law', Final Report of the Committee on the Formation of Customary Law, Conference Report London (2000).

Kishoiyan, B., 'The Utility of Bilateral Investment Treaties in the Formulation of Customary International Law' (1993) 14(2) Northwestern J. Int'l L.

Kill, T., 'Don't Cross the Streams: Past and Present Overstatement of Customary International Law in Connection with Conventional Fair and Equitable Treatment Obligations' (2008) 106 Michigan LR.

Kläger, Roland, *Fair and Equitable Treatment in International Investment Law* (Cambridge UP 2011).

Klein Bronfman, Marcela, 'Fair and Equitable Treatment: An Evolving Standard' (2006) 10 Max Planck Yrbk. UNL 624.

Laird, I., 'Betrayal, Shock and Outrage – Recent Developments in NAFTA Article 1105', in T. Weiler (ed.), *NAFTA Investment Law and Arbitration: Past Issues, Current Practice, Future Prospects* (Transnational Publ., 2004).

Mayeda, Graham, 'Playing Fair: The Meaning of Fair and Equitable Treatment in Bilateral Investment Treaties' (2007) 41(2) J. World Trade 273–291, 280.

OECD, *Fair and Equitable Treatment Standard in International Investment Law* (2004) No. 2004/3 Working Papers on International Investment Law.

Orellana, M.A. 'International Law on Investment: The Minimum Standard of Treatment (MST)' (2004) 3 Transnational Disp. Mgmt. 1–2.

Orakhelashvili, Alexander, 'The Normative Basis of "Fair and Equitable Treatment": General International Law on Foreign Investment?' (2008) 1 Archive des Völkerrechts.

Paparinskis, Martins, *The International Minimum Standard and Fair and Equitable Treatment* (Oxford UP 2013).

Paradell, L., 'The BIT Experience of The Fair And Equitable Treatment Standard', in Federico Ortino et al (eds), *Investment Treaty Law, Current Issues II* (British IICL 2007).

Paulsson, Jan, 'Neer-lv Misled?' Miami Law Research Paper 247 (see also: J. Paulsson & G. Petrochilos, 'Neer-ly Misled?' (2007) 22(2) ICSID Rev. 242–257).

Picherack, J. Roman, 'The Expanding Scope of the Fair and Equitable Treatment Standard: Have Recent Tribunals Gone Too Far?' (2008) 9(4) J. World Invest. & Trade.

Pinchis-Paulsen, Mona, 'The Life and Death (and Re-Birth) of "Fair and" "Equitable Treatment:" A Historical Examination of Twentieth Century International Trade and Investment Law Treaty-Making and Political Decision-Making' (Ph.D. Thesis, University of London (King's College), 2017.

Roth, Andreas Hans, *The Minimum Standard of International Law Applied to Aliens*, La Haye: A.W. Sijthoff, 1949.

Schill, Stephan, 'Fair and Equitable Treatment as an Embodiment of the Rule of Law', in R. Hofmann & C. Tams (eds), *The International Convention on the Settlement of Investment Disputes (ICSID): Taking Stock after 40 Years* (Nomos 2007).

Schreuer, C., 'Fair and Equitable Standard (FET): Interaction with Other Standards', (2007) 4(5) TDM.

Schreuer, C. 'Fair and Equitable Treatment in Arbitral Practice', (2005) 6 J. World Invest. & Trade.

Schwebel, Stephen M., 'Is Neer far from Fair and Equitable?' (2011) 27(4) Arb. Int'l 555–561.

Sornarajah, M., 'The Fair and Equitable Standard of Treatment: Whose Fairness? Whose Equity?' in Federico Ortino et al. (eds), *Investment Treaty Law: Current Issues II* (BIICL 2007).

Thomas, J.C., 'Reflections on Article 1105 of NAFTA: History, State Practice and the Influence of Commentators' (2002) 17(1) ICSID Rev.

Tudor, Ioana, *The Fair and Equitable Treatment Standard in International Foreign Investment Law* (Oxford UP 2008).

UNCTAD, *Fair and Equitable Treatment,* UNCTAD Series on Issues in International Investment Agreements (1999).

UNCTAD, *Fair and Equitable Treatment,* (2012) UNCTAD Series on Issues in International Investment Agreements II.

Vasciannie, Stephen, 'The Fair and Equitable Treatment Standard in International Investment Law and Practice' (1999) 70 British YIL 99.

Vandevelde, Kenneth J., 'A Unified Theory of Fair and Equitable Treatment' (2010) 43 NYU J. Int'l L. & Pol.

Weiler, Todd, *The Interpretation of International Investment Law: Equality, Discrimination and Minimum Standards of Treatment in Historical Context* (Martinus Nijhoff 2013).

Weiler, Todd, 'An Historical Analysis of the Function of the Minimum Standard of Treatment in International Investment Law' in Todd Weiler & Freya Baetens (eds.), *New Directions in International Economic Law: In Memoriam Thomas Wälde* (Martinus Nijhoff, 2011).

Yannaca-Small, Katia, 'Fair and Equitable Treatment Standard: Recent Developments', in A. Reinisch (ed), *Standards of Investment Protection*, (Oxford UP 2008).

www.ingramcontent.com/pod-product-compliance
Lightning Source LLC
Chambersburg PA
CBHW031332230926
51848CB00001B/202
9789004366114